W9-BNL-217

INSIDE
EVERY
Woman

INSIDE EVERY *Woman*

Using the
10 Strengths
You Didn't Know
You Had to Get
the Career
and Life
You Want Now

VICKIE L. MILAZZO, RN, MSN, JD

John Wiley & Sons, Inc.

Grateful acknowledgment is made to *The New York Times* for permission to reprint a quotation from Kathy Murphy's February 2, 2001 article, "Helping Nurses Move from Hospitals to Law Offices."

Copyright © 2006 by Vickie L. Milazzo. All rights reserved.

Published by John Wiley & Sons, Inc., Hoboken, New Jersey.

Published simultaneously in Canada.

No part of this publication may be reproduced, stored in a retrieval system, or transmitted in any form or by any means, electronic, mechanical, photocopying, recording, scanning, or otherwise, except as permitted under Sections 107 or 108 of the 1976 United States Copyright Act, without either the prior written permission of the Publisher, or authorization through payment of the appropriate per-copy fee to the Copyright Clearance Center, Inc., 222 Rosewood Drive, Danvers, MA 01923, (978) 750-8400, fax (978) 646-8600, or on the web at www.copyright.com. Requests to the Publisher for permission should be addressed to the Permissions Department, John Wiley & Sons, Inc., 111 River Street, Hoboken, NJ 07030, (201) 748-6011, fax (201) 748-6008 or online at http://www.wiley.com/go/permissions.

Limit of Liability/Disclaimer of Warranty: While the publisher and author have used their best efforts in preparing this book, they make no representations or warranties with respect to the accuracy or completeness of the contents of this book and specifically disclaim any implied warranties of merchantability or fitness for a particular purpose. No warranty may be created or extended by sales representatives or written sales materials. The advice and strategies contained herein may not be suitable for your situation. You should consult with a professional where appropriate. Neither the publisher nor author shall be liable for any loss of profit or any other commercial damages, including but not limited to special, incidental, consequential, or other damages.

This publication is designed to provide accurate and authoritative information in regard to the subject matter covered. It is sold with the understanding that the publisher is not engaged in rendering professional services. If legal, accounting, medical, psychological or any other expert assistance is required, the services of a competent professional person should be sought.

Designations used by companies to distinguish their products are often claimed as trademarks. In all instances where John Wiley & Sons, Inc. is aware of a claim, the product names appear in initial capital or all capital letters. Readers, however, should contact the appropriate companies for more complete information regarding trademarks and registration.

For general information on our other products and services please contact our Customer Care Department within the United States at (800) 762-2974, outside the United States at (317) 572-3993 or fax (317) 572-4002.

Wiley also publishes its books in a variety of electronic formats. Some content that appears in print may not be available in electronic books. For more information about Wiley products, visit our website at www.wiley.com.

ISBN-13: 978-0-471-74520-4
ISBN-10: 0-471-74520-0

Printed in the United States of America.

10 9 8 7 6 5 4

To my mom for setting me on my voyage of discovery,
to all the women exploring their extraordinary potential
and to my husband Tom for loving the woman
inside and outside me.

ACKNOWLEDGMENTS

The last thing I expected to bring home from a January speakers' conference in Cancun, Mexico was this book contract; perhaps sandy sneakers and sunburn, but not a July manuscript deadline. Somehow, in that crowded convention hall, my husband Tom found me refilling my cup with healthy green tea. He took my hand and led me away, telling me, "Skip your next session, there's someone you must meet." That someone turned out to be Matthew Holt, a patient, straight-talking editor at Wiley. After only two conversations Matt trusted me to be just as forthright as he is and believed in this book enough to share it with editor Emily Conway, who saw my vision and made this book possible.

Of course, it all started well before that sunny winter day. Everything in this book, everything I know and everything I love about being a woman comes from the amazing women and men in my life—starting with my mom and dad, Marise and Sal, my grandmother Mama Pearl and my sister Karen. My best friends Beth, Carol, Deb, Ellen, Jan, Missy and Nadia continue to teach me the power of fusion. My great teachers and mentors, especially my second mom, Blanche, all gave me models that I can only aspire to emulate.

Thanks to the Fusion women, Blanche, Chris, Evie, Jan, Leigh, Maggie, Martha and Susan, who inspired the Fusion and inspire me to attain the impossible.

I'd also like to thank the entire team at Vickie Milazzo Institute for their passion and for helping me create a business and story to write about and the thousands of CLNC®s, the Certified Legal Nurse Consultants, who have inspired me to live my 5 Promises as I help them to live theirs.

Thanks to Howard Caesar, my minister at Unity Church, who reminds me that life is good—all the time.

The following people helped me bring this book to life. Leigh Owen and Chris Rogers—you gave time, patience and massive amounts of red ink in teaching me everything you know about bringing words to paper. You are not only terrific mentors but awesome friends. I thank you both from the bottom of my heart. Special thanks also to Evie Baron-Hernandez, my fiery friend and sister from another life; Dana Zera, who laughed with me along the way; Lee F. Smith, who civilized my grammar barbarian tendencies; Maggie Kattan-Arroyos and Adrian Arroyos, who helped to bring visual form to the words; and especially Tom Ziemba, who gives me daily inspiration, is always there when my computer isn't and helped me rediscover some of the stories I'd almost forgotten.

Matt, next time we're in Cancun the margaritas are on me.

CONTENTS

5 PROMISES   *1*
*Make These Promises to Unleash the 10 Forces
Within You*

5 Promises Provide the Fuel   *3*

Promise 1: I Will Live and Work a Passionate Life   *4*

Promise 2: I Will Go for It or Reject It Outright   *5*

Promise 3: I Will Take One Action Step a Day Toward
My Passionate Vision   *7*

Promise 4: I Commit to Being a Success Student
for Life   *9*

Promise 5: I Believe as a Woman I Really Can
Do Anything   *10*

Harness Your 10 Feminine Forces with the 5 Promises   *11*

1 FIRE   *13*
Ignite Your Inner Fire to Live Passionately

Passion Fans the Flame of Success   *14*

Let Your Passions Move You   *16*

Discover Your Fire to Live Passionately   *17*

The Passionate Path Isn't Quick and Easy   *22*

Passion Doesn't Burn the Same for All Women   *24*

Nine Strategies for Living Passionately   *25*

Ignite Your Fire with the 5 Promises   33
Evie's Fire   35

2 INTUITIVE VISION   37
Imagine Unlimited Possibilities to Capture Your Vision

Order Off the Right Menu   39
Show Up with No Guarantee   41
Silence Arouses Imagination   42
Trust Your Way Through the Chaos   45
Imagination Trumps Knowledge   47
Accelerate Achievement with Hypnagogic Imagery   51
Hitch Your Vision to Your Passion   52
Be Ready with Your Next Vision   53
Capture Your Intuitive Vision with the 5 Promises   55
Maggie's Vision   57

3 ENGAGEMENT   59
Engage Commitment to Achieve Big Things

Ditch Perfectionism   61
Engage Your Fears to Conquer Them   63
Break the "Feel-Good" Addiction   66
Engage One Big Thing at a Time   68
Engage in What's Right, Not What's Easy   71
Engage the Details   72
Shrug Off Restrictions   74
Be Your Own Lottery   75
Don't Be a Commitment Queen   76

Engage to Achieve Big Things with the 5 Promises   *77*

Leigh's Engagement   *79*

4 AGILITY   *83*
Flex Your Agility to Grab New Opportunities

Shake It Up   *85*

Flex Your Curiosity   *86*

Challenge a Fixed Viewpoint   *89*

Stretch to Intensify Agility   *91*

Dive Deeper Every Day   *92*

Agility Is a Two-Minute Investment   *93*

Schedule an Agility Break   *95*

Don't Be a Relic of Past Splendor   *96*

Leave Your Old Comforts at Home   *98*

Flex Your Agility with the 5 Promises   *99*

Blanche's Agility   *101*

5 GENIUS   *103*
Intensify Your Intelligence for Accelerated Success

Women Ingeniously Collaborate   *104*

Collaboration Is Collective Genius   *105*

Genius Hears Other Voices   *107*

Remove Your Own Burrs   *108*

Genius Is Trusting Your Own Voice   *109*

Genius Multiplies Itself   *111*

Genius Combines IQ and Hard Work   *113*

Employ the Genius of Einstein   *114*

Intensify Your Genius with the 5 Promises   *119*

Chris's Genius   *121*

6 INTEGRITY   **125**
Practice Uncompromising Integrity for
Authentic Success

Breaching Integrity Betrays Opportunity   *127*

Every Act Counts   *128*

Consensus on Integrity Is Elusive   *129*

Every Promise Counts   *135*

Put Your Integrity Where Your Mouth Is   *137*

Do the Right Thing When No One Is Looking   *138*

Refuse to Be an Integrity Victim   *139*

Avoid the Lure of Manipulation   *140*

Live Authentic Success   *141*

Practice Uncompromising Integrity with the 5 Promises   *144*

Jan's Integrity   *146*

7 ENDURANCE   **149**
Fuel Your Endurance to Energize Your Performance

Keep Dancing Your Passionate Vision   *151*

Fuel Your Endurance with Persistence   *153*

Fuel Endurance with Incremental Payoffs   *155*

Fuel Endurance with the Right Focus   *157*

Endure for the Fun of It   *158*

Take to the Air Like a Butterfly   *160*

Fuel Your Endurance with Fire   *161*

Harvest Energy to Increase Your Endurance   *163*

10 Strategies for Building Your Endurance Muscles   *165*

Fuel Your Endurance with the 5 Promises   *167*

Susan's Endurance   *169*

8   ENTERPRISE   *171*
Become the CEO of Your Career and Life

Be First at the River to Get a Drink   *172*

Satisfy Your Thirst at the River of Choice   *174*

Venture Out from a Solid Foundation   *179*

Assemble an Extraordinary Framework   *186*

Act Like a CEO   *187*

Become the CEO of Your Career and Life
with the 5 Promises   *194*

Martha's Enterprise   *196*

9   RENEWAL   *199*
Reclaim Your Life Energy Through Frequent Renewal

Renew Your Relationship with Yourself   *201*

Renew Your Physical Energy Daily   *202*

Replenish Your Emotional Energy   *205*

Nurture and Renew Your Spirit   *211*

Recharge Your Mental Energy   *212*

Celebrate to Intensify Renewal   *214*

Renew Your Energy with the People You Love   *215*

Renew by Giving Back   *217*

Six Additional Strategies for Total Renewal   *218*

Reclaim Your Life Energy with the 5 Promises   *220*

Lindsay's Renewal   *222*

10 FEMALE FUSION 225
Fuse with Incredible Women to Attain
the Impossible

The Story of the First Female Fusion 226

Three Stories of Women Forever Changed 230

Female Fusion Is a Protective Caprock 235

Fusion Is More Than a Women's Group 236

Fusion Needs Heat 236

Female Fusion Requires Purpose 237

The Basic Fusion Format Is Simple 239

Activate Your First Fusion 241

Spark Fusion Throughout the Entire Group 243

Unleash Boundless Fusion Energy 246

Have Fun with Fusion as You Attain the Impossible 248

Activate Female Fusion with the 5 Promises 250

Vickie's Fusion 252

Inside Every Woman Is a Lifelong Adventure 255

About the Author 257

A woman is the full circle. Within her is the power to create,
nurture and transform.
—Diane Mariechild

The bolder your promises, the richer your bounty.
—Vickie L. Milazzo

5 $\mathscr{P}$ROMISES

Make These Promises to Unleash the 10 Forces Within You

What would your life look like if every moment of it was absolutely enriched, fulfilled and swelling with joy? Think about it—your health, relationships, career, spirituality and finances are the best they can be and you greet each day with energy and enthusiasm for whatever comes your way. What would accomplish that?

This book is about finding your way to that place through 5 Promises that will unleash 10 extraordinary strengths inside of you.

I discovered the 5 Promises in 1982 when I faced the reality that I was unhappy with the direction my life was taking. It wasn't easy after putting hard work into becoming a registered nurse (RN), earning my bachelor's degree and my master's degree, and working six years in the hospital, to find I was extremely disappointed by the career choice I had made. I'd gone in wide-eyed, thinking I could make a difference, even improve the state of healthcare, only to bump up against the reality that no matter how hard I worked, my efforts would never make a dent, much less an impact. I was also moving far too slowly toward financial success, and I was forgetting what it was like to have fun on the job.

A quick look at my colleagues who had been in this career for 20 years or more showed me that my future held more of the same. Not that they weren't trying really hard, but their passion for nursing had died. I could see that my passion was starting to die too and wondered if I might be wasting my potential.

Refusing to accept such a dismal outlook, I made five promises to myself. They became the 5 Promises I have continued to renew daily for more than two decades, and which changed not only my career but my entire life.

They opened me up to 10 extraordinary strengths inside every woman. The 5 Promises and 10 Feminine Forces have worked for me through all the passages of my development, from realizing I wanted something beyond traditional nursing to building a $12 million enterprise. They still work for me today. They can do the same for you if you commit to follow them.

How do I know there aren't just a few women graced with such awesome forces? As a hospital nurse I had the opportunity to work side by side with ordinary women performing extraordinary feats countless times a day. For 24 years I've trained real women to combine their 10 Feminine Forces with their professional expertise to achieve unreal success. I guarantee that none of these women has anything you don't have. My company employs more women than men, so I've been on both the mentoring side and the receiving side of the extraordinary feminine forces you'll explore throughout this book. Women's strengths continue to help grow my company and have been a big reason for its success.

I love women. I love men, too—especially my husband Tom—but I find so many more unexplored possibilities in working with the feminine energy.

5 PROMISES PROVIDE THE FUEL

With these 5 Promises I have built a successful, challenging, continuously evolving business I love while enjoying relationships that reward me constantly with joy. Although it may seem unlikely, I rise each morning overflowing with excitement and with the physical, mental and emotional energy I need to accomplish a remarkably busy schedule. I even manage to find time for myself almost every day. While these are not the only secrets to my success, I would not be where I am today if I hadn't made and kept these essential promises.

No two women are alike in lifestyle, social upbringing or earthly desires, yet we do share certain strengths. Inside every woman is an amazing fire that, when fueled, can release volcanic potential. And in my years of experience in stirring that fire for uncounted women, I've discovered that summoning the phenomenal power of your 10 Feminine Forces through the 5 Promises will enable you to attain any future you envision.

Sometimes we make a promise, set about reaching a goal, and we do it, but then it's over. That's not what this book is about. It isn't a magic formula, a quick fix for success. It's a life plan for using the 10 strengths you didn't know you had to get the career and life you want now—and for as long as you choose to use it. It's a pattern for achieving anything you want, a pattern to use over and over for as long as your dreams are supported by discipline and commitment.

The courage to commit is easily within the grasp of every woman on this planet, including you. Begin unleashing the interconnected forces within you by making my 5 Promises *your* 5 Promises. When you do, they will guide you in directing your vision and will fan your flame of success.

PROMISE 1: I WILL LIVE AND WORK A PASSIONATE LIFE

We all know when we discover something we feel passionate about. We feel amazingly energetic. Desire is energy. Have you ever experienced a time when desire overcame all physical, emotional and intellectual barriers? Like a child waking up on Christmas morning, you spring alert full speed ahead. Why can't we experience that passion—that vitality and energy—not only on Christmas but every day? Believe me, you can. When you wake up every day to a life and career that are your heart and soul, a life and career you're passionate about, you experience maximum joy.

One of my passions was ignited in me when I was eight years old. For hours each day I taught an imaginary class. I was so absorbed with my class that my dad would come in and break it up to encourage me to play outside with my real friends. To this day I have no idea what I was teaching, but I was darned passionate about it.

At eight years old teaching was play. At 28, I turned that passion for teaching into a business, and I've been playing ever since. When I left hospital nursing to start my legal nurse consulting business, I promised myself I would work only my passions. That decision proved more important than I realized. Along the way I've been tempted by many flattering and interesting offers, the most tempting of which was joining a powerful law firm as a partner my first year out of law school. But I always stop and listen to my heart. When we live and work our passions, we take an uncompromising approach. It means being honest with ourselves and others about what we value.

Writing this book was a passion for me, although at times it felt tedious. Passion is more than an emotion, it's a strength you build, a strength that provides a platform for everything you want to achieve.

As *The New York Times* reported, I "crossed nursing with the law and created a new profession" when I started teaching other nurses how to become legal nurse consultants. That's the kind of Big Thing that can happen when you commit to Promise 1, to living and working a passionate life.

Commit to this first promise right now and use the ideas in this book to make it happen. Don't worry if you have no clue what your passions are, exactly. As you read this book and work the exercises, you'll discover the passions that will propel you to a totally fulfilled future.

PROMISE 2: I WILL GO FOR IT OR REJECT IT OUTRIGHT

If you want something better for your life and career, you owe it to yourself to go for it or reject it outright. Don't leave the dream dangling as a reminder of what you don't have the time, courage or enthusiasm to grab. Do it or forget it.

Don't wait for the conditions to be perfect. That will never happen. People who wait or dabble usually end up at their retirement party rewarded with a glass of watery punch and a piece of white cake. Own up to your passions, then step out and grab hold of them with both hands.

Despite a fear of cliff-hanging heights, I stepped out of an airplane at 14,000 feet to skydive. I was terrified. Once out of the plane's cabin I couldn't step back in. I was truly committed, even if not by choice, and the exhilaration I felt later at overcoming that lifelong fear proved to be a catalyst for future accomplishments.

Most of us stay in the safe cabin of everyday life. We never step out into the audacious dreams that smolder and spark inside us. What would your life look like if you didn't have the choice of that safe cabin? If your only option was to grab that dream and jump into it? To go all the way once you made the jump?

Fear will freeze you in place. Don't tell yourself, "One day, some day, I might get around to living my dreams." With that attitude, one day, some day, you're sipping that retirement punch regretting all the things you didn't do.

Many of the women I mentor won't "go for it" because of their fears. One thing that helps me go for it is perspective. My mom Marise gave me that. She had a dream of traveling far beyond New Orleans, where I grew up. She read books that took her to the Eiffel Tower, Big Ben and the Sistine Chapel, and she planned on visiting all of them. Then she met my dad. She often said, "When we have enough money, we'll travel." But then she had children, and she said, "When the kids are grown and out of the house, then we'll travel." Then the kids were out of the house and my mom died—at age 48—from breast cancer. Her travel dreams never came true.

What are you waiting for to live your dreams? What are you waiting for to have a life of passion? When you get enough money? When you lose enough weight? When your business is perfect? When your spouse is perfect?

My mom's death taught me that the time is now. When I'm afraid to take a risk, which is quite often, I honor my mom by asking myself, "What's the worst thing that can happen?" The perspective of knowing it's not cancer or death helps me to do the thing I fear.

It's perfectly okay to admit that a commitment is not right for you and to reject it outright. This is your life, your passionate future.

What's not okay is to hold back and put less than everything into a commitment that is your passion. If you want something, go for it all the way and go for it now. When you do, you'll wake up every day to a life and career you love.

PROMISE 3: I WILL TAKE ONE ACTION STEP A DAY TOWARD MY PASSIONATE VISION

Dreams and visions are great, but without action they are nothing more than hallucinations. Without action your visions scud away and dissolve like clouds. I've met many people much smarter than I am who had dreams and ideas but didn't do anything with them. They didn't take action.

When a national news anchor from CNN asked me how I got to where I am today, in light of my humble beginnings, I was hoping to say something profound. But the truth was I did it one step at a time. I grew up in a hardworking blue-collar household—actually, it was a "no-collar" household because in New Orleans, with no air conditioning, we wore T-shirts. I worked to put myself through nursing school, and I was proud of that accomplishment. But I wanted more. After only six years in nursing I looked at my future and I saw that it wasn't for me. I envisioned beyond the horizon an alternate world where the medical and legal worlds merged, a world as a legal nurse consultant.

That world did not yet exist, but I believed I could make it so. And while belief in my vision was crucial, belief alone wasn't enough. I needed to take action to realize that vision.

Like anyone trying to accomplish any whopping big goal, I had to tackle it in small workable chunks—talk to that first attorney, get my first project and build my first client relationship. Most important, I had to take action every single day.

I lacked business savvy, but with each small step I gained both knowledge and momentum. Sometimes I barreled through with enthusiasm, other times I could barely convince myself to inch forward, but the accumulated effect of all those steps brought me to where I am today. What I learned in the process and what still applies now is that it is less important *what* I do and more important that I *do something*.

I acted on a breakthrough idea in my profession. Anyone could have done the same—and I know other nurses may have had similar ideas—but what separated me from those others was that I took the action steps necessary to realize my dream. Ideas are important, but success is in the motion.

Successful women love the action as much as the dream. By taking action every day you develop the habit and discipline to make your vision a reality. When you focus not just on the idea but on making it happen, you stay in motion, not just dreaming your passions but living them.

Make this third promise now, that you will take at least one action step every day for the next 30 days on the big thing that will bring you closer to your passionate visions in a big way. Once you are hooked on the natural high of action, taking giant leaps comes easy.

PROMISE 4: I COMMIT TO BEING A SUCCESS STUDENT FOR LIFE

All great athletes and performers practice every day. Even after they achieve a level of success, they continue to practice and take instruction from their coaches, learning new ways to reach higher levels. They are lifetime students.

Success breeds success. Becoming a success student for life is about practicing being successful. What's hard today is easy tomorrow—with practice.

A woman who started her business after completing our certification program told me, "I think I can do this." A few weeks later, when the demands of the business world had her spinning in circles, she called and told me, "No way I can do this." We talked through some of the strategies she had learned in class, and she kept taking action steps. When she accomplished her first big business goal, she called me again. This time she said, "I know I can do this."

It is a myth to think you can launch a successful career or succeed in other life goals without learning, even if your driving desire is as intuitive as being a full-time mom. Successful women respect the complexity of any chosen path and become students for life.

I've been in business for over two decades, and I still learn every day—from my students, staff members, favorite writers, speakers and business experts. No matter what the subject, there is always more to learn.

There are two ways you can learn:

✦ The hard way—through trial and error, making lots of mistakes. You're going to do some of that anyway, but this is a slow, expensive path to success.

✦ The easier way—through the experience of others who have already successfully overcome the problems and discovered the answers. This is the quick and sure path to success. Just about any problem you will encounter, the right mentor has already successfully managed. And mentors come in many forms, from family members, friends and colleagues to books, CDs and Internet resources.

As a committed lifetime student, I choose to listen and learn from mentors who are far more successful than I am, many who have never met me. I attribute much of my success to choosing my mentors wisely.

Commit now to being a lifetime student and to learning not only from your own mistakes and accomplishments but also from successful mentors. When you do so, "I think I can" becomes "I know I can," squelching any thoughts of "No way I can."

PROMISE 5: I BELIEVE AS A WOMAN I REALLY CAN DO ANYTHING

I was lucky to go to an all-girls high school. Coed schools have advantages, too, but when I grew up men were expected to be the business geniuses, women to be helpful homemakers. I gained confidence in those formative years from not having teachers telling me the boys were smarter or calling on them instead of me. As a young woman I honestly believed I could do anything. Believing you can do it is 90 percent of the win.

Any time I have hesitated to go for it, it was because I had stopped believing in myself the way I did in those glorious adolescent years. Today, when an opportunity arises and I find myself hesitating, I remember, "I'm a woman. I can do anything." I think back to my past success as an RN in the hospital, making split-second decisions that were the difference between life and death for my patients. Then I remind myself: If I could save lives in the middle of the night while the rest of the world was sleeping and a doctor was nowhere in sight, surely I could make effective decisions in my career and life.

Find your own example, a personal or career accomplishment that gives you pride and encouragement, then use it to bolster your resolve. Any time you're not grabbing the opportunity, tell yourself, "I am a woman and I can do anything!"

HARNESS YOUR 10 FEMININE FORCES WITH THE 5 PROMISES

Commit with me to these 5 Promises right now, even if you're not yet sure how to incorporate them into your life. That's what this book will help you define. I guarantee that by just beginning this journey your life will become an adventure more powerful and satisfying than you can imagine. Whether you're aspiring to be an artist, engineer, homemaker, real estate agent or astronaut, or are already successful in your chosen field, these 5 Promises will help you harness your 10 Feminine Forces and propel you toward audacious success.

These forces—fire, intuitive vision, engagement, agility, genius, integrity, endurance, enterprise, renewal and fusion—are not purely women's domain. Men certainly exhibit many of them. But women synthesize these strengths in a potent energy that is distinctively female.

In creating this book, I assembled the first Female Fusion, a meeting of phenomenal women who shared their vision of how the feminine forces contributed to their success. You'll hear from these women at the end of each chapter. I encourage you to invite women who inspire, instruct, accept and honor you to read this book together and work through the 5 Promises. Collectively you will achieve even more momentum for getting the career and life you want now. Read Chapter 10, "Female Fusion," to learn how we did it and how to engage other women to accelerate your passionate journey to astonishing success.

Whichever approach you use, alone or with friends, the 10 Feminine Forces, harnessed by the 5 Promises, are all you need to succeed. Once you make the commitment, there is no limit to where you can go. You can experience new career adventures, enjoy more time with yourself and your family, and create a life you love in every way.

This proven life plan works. And it's easy. I'll walk you through it step by step. Start today—and embrace your amazing new life without limits.

Promise big and promise now!

I resolved to take fate by the throat and shake a living out of her.
—Louisa May Alcott

Well-behaved women rarely make history.
—Anita Borg

If you want the impossible done, give it to a woman on fire.
—Vickie L. Milazzo

$\mathscr{F}$IRE

Ignite Your Inner Fire to Live Passionately

Women are born passionate. We love hard. We cry hard. When we care about something passionately we can change the world.

Heroines who lived in times when strong women were not in vogue, such as French military leader Joan of Arc, American temperance reformer Carrie Nation, abolitionist Harriett Tubman and women's rights activist Margaret Sanger, changed the world because their passions drove them to stand strong for what they believed. Women have also carved out their place in the arts: dancer Isadora Duncan, blues singer Ella Fitzgerald, artist Georgia O'Keeffe, author Jane Austen. All passionately talented women—women like you.

Life is not about having or not having passion. All women have it inside. Either you honor that passion in your life, or you don't. Often we fear passion. We fear it won't stick, so we avoid it altogether. We fear that, like a lover, it will "betray us."

Every woman has the potential to dig deeper, to find the way to her passion and to live with fire. This won't make your life easier, but it will certainly make it more rewarding.

When I was growing up in a modest shotgun house in New Orleans, nothing about my childhood suggested I was destined to travel. Yet I was fascinated by it and dreamed of exploring the world. I wrote to foreign consuls and requested free information about their countries. I remember receiving big, colorful brochures—probably not as big or colorful as I recall. Those brochures were the only way I could experience my unrealized passion for travel. Each imaginary trip I took on paper was vivid and exciting.

Years later, when I became a nurse, there was little money or time for travel. But I found ways to indulge that passion. I attended one or two nursing conferences a year, choosing destinations that beckoned. I also traveled during my two-week vacation, no matter how tight my budget. These modest experiences made the passion inside me burn deeper, and when I eventually turned my passion for nursing into the business of legal nurse consulting, I included travel as part of my vision. Today, I enjoy not only passions for entrepreneurship, writing and teaching, but also my passion for travel. I have sipped yak butter tea with monks in the Himalayas, eaten sheep's brains with Berbers in Morocco and drained a gourd of grassy maté with gauchos on a Patagonian estancia. Because I consciously acknowledged and pursued my passions, I created a life that embraces all of them in some small way, including travel.

PASSION FANS THE FLAME OF SUCCESS

Without the fire that only passion arouses, success eludes us. If you're not passionate about an idea, you won't do what it takes to carry it out, because pursuing that idea would be way too hard without passion.

To be an expert rock climber, you have to push through the pain and discomfort of scraped hands and aching muscles to excel, and to do that you must have fervent passion for the sport. If you're passionate about your job, you'll be far more successful in advancing your career than a woman who isn't.

To live passionately is to act. If you're true to yourself, you'll put energy behind your passions and take the necessary actions to bring them to fulfillment. You make time for the fire that burns inside you.

I'm lucky that as a child I played at teaching imaginary classes for free and now get to earn real money doing it. Work, for me, is still passionate play. But what if you're not sure what your one passion is? Does that mean you'll never find it? No, because passion is not just one thing, not just a career, a cause or a relationship. Passion is a way of approaching and enjoying life to the fullest. The gain is the passion itself, not a prize of victory, more money or more friends, although such rewards may well follow.

Passions are driven by a variety of values and beliefs. A woman can be passionate about excellence, like Carol, the education director who is as passionate about creating the perfect policy and procedure manual as she is about planning a conference for more than 1,400 people. One woman's passion for a healthy body can result in dedication to a workout that another woman would consider drudgery. Passion can be an intention to accomplish a goal, such as getting a promotion or being recognized by your peers.

Passions change and evolve. At any given time passion is a choice, and what you're passionate about is a choice. A woman can be passionate about anything she goes after (although my husband often reminds me that straightening the magazines on the rack and folding a perfect hospital corner on our bed are compulsions, not passions). My friend Yvonne was passionately immersed in her career. Then she had a child she hadn't planned for, and now she's equally passionate about raising, teaching and loving that child.

Passions are lived out in as many expressions as there are women. Yours are inside you, and they will reveal themselves if you listen carefully.

LET YOUR PASSIONS MOVE YOU

We all know there's no one magic formula for prosperity and happiness, but there's one common denominator I've found among successful women: They have a passionate drive to do what they do. They're on fire. Some inner spark in the mind, spirit and soul burns intensely, driving them over seemingly insurmountable barriers. Passionate women don't do what they do just because they can—they do it because they are irresistibly compelled.

Alicia Alonso, the Cuban ballerina, is recognized as one of the finest classical ballerinas of our time. Her achievement is all the more impressive because Alicia is one woman we probably should never have heard of. Her soul was fired up to dance, but her body wasn't cooperating.

At 19, when she was not yet a famous dancer, Alicia was diagnosed with a detached retina. Her condition required three successive operations and left her with partial sight but no peripheral vision. After surgery Alicia was instructed to lie in bed, perfectly still, for a year. But Alicia's flame would not be extinguished by mere physical limitation. During her year of enforced bed rest she danced in her mind and with her toes to keep her feet, memory and passion alive. She taught herself to dance *Giselle,* a difficult ballet that demands the ballerina's full dramatic range.

When Alicia returned to the stage every prop and light was placed exactly the same for every performance, so that she could memorize her moves and dance even with her limited vision. The deadly peril of the orchestra pit awaited her slightest misstep or memory lapse. Still, Alicia Alonso achieved world renown and was honored with the highest designation a ballerina can earn, *Prima Ballerina Assoluta*.

Was it only talent that made her one of the world's most successful ballerinas? Or was it her driving passion to do what she loved despite overwhelming odds?

DISCOVER YOUR FIRE TO LIVE PASSIONATELY

If your passions have not yet got you leaping into action, try the following exercises to coax them to the surface. And please, write in this book. This book is yours. By putting your thoughts here, you personalize it and make it your guiding companion.

1. *Connect with your early interests.* Can you recall a pleasant childhood memory of playing? If so, what is it? What comes to mind first? *Write it down, no matter how absurd. It could make sense to you later, even if it does not make sense now.*

   _____

   _____

   _____

   _____

   When you think about this play scenario, ask yourself: Did you love it? Were you passionate? Were you good at it? Did you engage in it every chance you could, without being pushed? Did your parents have to drag you away from it? *Now, describe it.*

_____

_____

_____

_____

Perhaps your memory comes from your teen years or early adulthood. Or it might be the first time you recognized a special talent, developed a latent skill or derived pure pleasure from an accomplishment. If you can remember even one time in your life when you felt passionately excited and no one had to push you into action, then you know how to ignite your passion for success. Write down something, even if you aren't quite certain or it seems outrageous.

2. *Acknowledge your current interests.* Imagine you have all the money you need and nine months to do anything and everything you want to do—pursue any career or hobby, live in a new state or country, sing with your favorite band or climb Mount Everest. You will be free of worry about financial or practical matters during that entire time. What would you do? Take three minutes to stretch your imagination and write down everything, but do not limit your answers to the obvious, such as traveling or spending more time with family and friends. *Write fast and write as many things as you can think of. When your three minutes are up, stop.*

_____

_____

_____

_____

Glance quickly over your list. You'll notice that a few items give you a profound feeling of excitement, urgency or even disappointment. *Circle three that ignite a spark.*

Next, considering your everyday world as it exists right now, list everything you might want to accomplish in the next year. Stop after two minutes and circle three items that spark the most passion inside you.

_____

_____

_____

_____

_____

3. *Go inside, listen and choose your actions.* Thinking back to when I was a child, I see that much of what I was passionate about has become a big part of my life now. It didn't happen instantly, but eventually I reconnected with those childhood passions and incorporated them into my adult life. In the process I had to make choices.

   Women tend to pile on the responsibilities. Why buy into the myth that we must handle it all—home, children, career, care of an aging parent, social obligations, financial wizardry—and still have energy for great sex? Listen to your inner voice and you know that myth is ridiculous. Yes, we probably can handle it all—we're women, we can do anything—but why should we? Men would never expect to juggle so many responsibilities.

   My good friend who is 60 has been cooking breakfast and dinner her entire married life. When her husband retired, he wanted her to make lunch, too. At first she hopped in and did it. But soon it grated on her that his retirement meant she had more work to do. Preparing another meal was contrary to her passion for enjoying life, so she decided to retrain her husband. She told him, "Our wedding vows included better or worse but not lunch. You're on your own for lunch."

How many of the everyday responsibilities in your life can be eliminated? Or delegated? Or hired out? Or automated? Which responsibilities no longer support you? Let them go. Eliminating just one or two items from your busy schedule can free up time to pursue your passionate interests. *Write down two responsibilities you will no longer handle personally.*

_____

_____

_____

_____

4. ***Keep listening and quickly reject whatever you're not passionate about.*** We all go through stages where our energy comes from a particular source, and once that source no longer provides a driving vitality, it's okay to let go and ignite a new fire.

There was a time when I loved to cook. I was passionate about cooking. I loved preparing a meal and having friends over to eat it. Now I'm just as happy eating out. I'd rather relax with my friends without the bother of kitchen duty. For a while I felt guilty and thought I should still love cooking. Finally, the epiphany—I don't have to be passionate about cooking anymore. While that fire burned inside me, I did it, I loved it. Then other passions took over and I moved on. When a passion burns out, let it go.

And if your burning passions are not yet evident, rejecting everything you clearly are not passionate about can help you get closer. Try backing into your passions with the following exercise.

Look at what you absolutely don't want to do. "I don't want to do this, or this. . . ." *Write down five things you absolutely don't want to do.*

_____

_____

_____

_____

Then write down five things you might not mind doing.
"Maybe I would like to do this . . . or this."

_____

_____

_____

_____

Eventually you'll hit on something that speaks to you:
"Yes . . . I could really enjoy doing this." Is that a passion?
Maybe, maybe not. Only by exploring it will you know. *For
now, write it down.*

_____

_____

_____

_____

Be patient. If you don't get a fire in the belly that feels like
real passion, keep exploring. Maybe for now it's only a tiny
spark. The flame has to start somewhere.

5. *Foresee the reality of your passions.* Frequently we want a result
without foreseeing the full implications of that result. Fame
brings intense responsibility and an end to privacy. Breaking a
record opens the door to all contenders.

Alice wanted to be a keynote speaker until she saw the lifestyle that keynoting represented—living out of a suitcase, sleeping in musty hotels away from home and loved ones. She was
able to modify that passion without forsaking her passion for
family by speaking locally with only occasional trips out of town.

Suzi dreamed of opening a bed and breakfast and playing host to new guests every day. Soon after opening, she found that her time was spent cleaning, cooking, washing dishes, invoicing and answering the reservation line. That reality wasn't what she signed up for, so she changed it by hiring a manager and staff. Now she enjoys her dream of entertaining guests without toilet duty.

What benefit will you gain by living your passions? What are the realities of that lifestyle? Does this passion support your other life goals? If not, how can you modify or merge them?

_____

_____

_____

_____

_____

THE PASSIONATE PATH ISN'T QUICK AND EASY

After I became an independent legal nurse consultant, I went to law school at night. I was consulting with a group of attorneys who, after I graduated, offered me a position as an associate attorney. I graciously and easily declined, thinking, "Why would I want to do that? I'm doing what I love, having more freedom and making more money than any new associate." A year later a partner at the law firm approached me and said, "Okay, if you won't come on as an associate, we're inviting you to be a partner."

This attractive offer raised the stakes considerably. Suddenly, saying yes to my passion wasn't so easy. I loved consulting with these attorneys, and a partnership would guarantee a bigger and brighter future every year, financially and in other respects.

But after the rosy glow of ego gratification dimmed, I declined the offer. Practicing law was not my passion, even with such ideal conditions. Eventually, choosing passion paid off big, although the payoff came more slowly. My passion was so strong that my business soon soared despite my lack of business training or education. I surpassed the law firm's offer in every way and was able to maintain my freedom, create my own financial security and, most of all, enjoy the career I'm passionate about.

That kind of decision isn't easy. What's easy is to compromise, say yes to a lukewarm interest because we, or someone else, think it's a smarter decision. Live and work your passions and the reward will come, maybe not always financially, but in a way that matters to you.

Daryn Kagan, news anchor for CNN, knew at age 16 she wanted a job that would be different every day. Her first thought, to become a doctor, lasted only through a single chemistry class, but her second childhood vision, to be a television reporter, became her driving passion. After five and a half years at a local TV station, she asked to move up to anchor. Repeatedly her boss passed her over to hire blondes. "There's just this 'it,'" he told her, "and some people have it and some don't. Clearly, you don't."

That was harsh, but Daryn refused to let her boss define her direction, her passion or her success. She circumvented his limiting beliefs and forged her own path. She convinced him to put her on as weekend morning sportscaster, a position she invented, and for over a year she worked that job for free. Daryn, who had a passion for sports, saw this as a way to get noticed at a much higher level—since this was a field where women were not the norm. Later, when a position opened up at CNN, she got it, and after only three years became an anchor.

It would have been so easy for Daryn to believe her first boss's assessment of her future in television. Similarly, it would have been easy for me to believe my peers' assessment that the unsatisfactory healthcare system was the best place for a nurse's expertise. Sometimes the smartest move is to move on, especially when it's obvious that no matter what you do there's no reward at the end. Don't let others define you, your passion or your direction. When Daryn's passion was tested, she paid her dues, then moved on, following her own path and reaching the outcome she desired. When my passion was tested I created my own profession, where I could make a difference and make big things happen.

By following my passion and my 5 Promises, I was fortunate to get both financial reward and a life I love. You can, too.

PASSION DOESN'T BURN THE SAME FOR ALL WOMEN

Not everyone feels and expresses passion in the same way. Being Italian, I tend toward the active, fire-in-the-belly, excited way of seeing and doing things. My husband says I'm like a summer storm. I blow in, there's thunder, lightning, wind and rain, then I blow out.

My Vietnamese housekeeper, Thi Thu, is the calmest person in the world. She's unflappable, but I know she's passionate about cooking. She arranges shrimp on a plate around a sculptured mound of seasoned rice with all their tails pointing just so. Her salads are mosaic perfections, every vegetable cut precisely and layered in bands of color. When I make a salad, I chop it up any old way I can and toss it all together. It's food. Clean it and eat it. Her dishes are works of art. Mine are works of sustenance. Anyone can tell by the results that she loves preparing meals, but watching her go about it with such amazing calm you'd never recognize her passion.

It's okay if your passion burns differently. What's important is that the fire burns bright for you.

NINE STRATEGIES FOR LIVING PASSIONATELY

In March 1982, I had the privilege of seeing Alicia Alonso dance. She was 61 years old. I had no doubt that her passionate drive accounted for her long, successful career. That same month I started my business. This woman and her unflagging energy have inspired me ever since.

We are measured not by how we deal with victory and accomplishment, but by how we deal with failure and disappointment. When life gets tough, I remember Alicia and other passionate women like her whose blazing fire wouldn't be stifled.

Nine Ways to Live Passionately

1. *Commit to the fire.* We live in an increasingly passive society today, where we can sit and watch the news, play video games or chat on the Internet and believe we're involved when all we're doing is idling in place while life passes us by. We're not doing much, yet it seems like we're doing a lot.

   Passivity is dangerous to passion, because passion never resides in a passive house. A passionate woman doesn't wait on the sofa. She's awake and moving. When a scintillating opportunity appears she seizes it on the spot.

2. *Practice being fiery.* If you're thinking, "I'm not naturally passionate," don't despair. You can practice passion as easily as you can practice any sport. Start by approaching your day and your life with positive energy. Any negative energy will interfere with expressing your passion.

   I had never even been to a hockey game until my husband dragged me to one "kicking and screaming." We sat behind the goal, protected by a glass barrier, and within minutes I was into it. I didn't know the rules, didn't understand what was happen-

ing down on that ice, but I was beating on the glass, yelling
at the players, the goalies, the referees, the people around me,
"kicking and screaming" and having the time of my life. I was
practicing passion—at least, that's what I told Tom.

It takes practice to be passionate, just as it takes practice to
excel at any endeavor. Any time you feel as if you're not living
passionately, try to enjoy what's happening anyway. We can't
skip the parts of life we don't enjoy, and few of us can enjoy
every single moment. I have a friend who runs five miles a day,
even in rain or sleet, and when I mistakenly mentioned that
she loves to run, she quickly corrected me. "I don't love running, I love the benefits of running. All the while I'm out there
I tell myself how good it will feel when I stop." I had no idea
she didn't love running.

You have two choices about every moment you live: You
can appreciate the experience and at least learn from it, or you
can be miserable. Choose the positive road. Nothing destroys
passion quicker than negativity. "I'm passionate about hip-
hop singing but I hate my day job" is not the energy that will
propel you to succeed in that day job until you can quit to
pursue your passion for hip-hop. It's okay to know you're in
a temporary way station, but be happy in your way station.
Find at least one aspect of your job to be passionate about. No
experience is a waste; it's training for what comes next.

Practice passion in every situation and make everything
you do your passion training ground.

3. *Do something, even if it's wrong.* Ninety percent of success is
showing up. Whether you're selling an idea, trying to land a
new job or learning to paint, the bottom line is that you have
to show up and dance. Many people are afraid to commit to a
passion because they feel that a firecracker has to go off, a light

has to shine or a voice from the heavens has to proclaim, "This is it!" Maybe that firecracker will pop, maybe not.

And what you're passionate about today may arouse no interest tomorrow. At any given time new passions emerge and you evolve differently.

Yet, even when you recognize that your passion today might not be your passion tomorrow, that it's okay to move on, committing to one path as opposed to another is often difficult. Do something anyway, even if it's wrong.

4. *Light your own fire.* My dad is 81 years old. Sal has had two heart attacks and two bypass surgeries, and he has outlived two wives. Based on statistical probability he's pretty much "out of warranty," but keeps going and going and going because he has a reason for waking up every morning. My dad's passionate about playing poker at a local casino to the point that I have to call him at a specific time or miss him entirely. He's not a big gambler; he rarely wins or loses more than $30 a day and usually ends the week even. You and I might shake our heads at such a passion, but it keeps him young and feisty.

Likewise, don't be disappointed if others don't get your passion. It doesn't matter whether your passion satisfies anybody else. This is your life, your passion, not theirs.

Too often we buy into other people's definition of what's right or wrong, where we should or shouldn't go. Stop being so well-behaved. I'm not suggesting we arbitrarily break rules. We need to know what has worked and failed to work in the past. But rules can also serve as constraints, holding you back from achieving your passionate success.

My motto is "I do it my way—you got a problem with that?" That motto helps me to live my fire, not everyone else's. My way doesn't always work, but at the end of the day,

I'm comfortable failing if I know I followed my own passion rather than someone else's.

Don't just break rules, make your own rules. A woman in my company is practically combustible. She has been setting fires all over our office since her first day. She accepts the responsibilities of her job while constantly making new rules and brilliantly gaining acceptance for them. She has completely rewritten her job description and is passionately involved in every aspect of the company. What new rule would you have to make to light your own bonfire?

5. *Ignite your fire with a spark.* Women often think their passion is not worthy, that it should be bigger, bolder, more important. No one pushed me to do great things while growing up, but I am thankful my family taught me to be passionate about little things like touch football, powdered sugar fights at Café du Monde and card games that cost me my allowance.

Sparks ignite fires. Only you can decide which spark is worthy of your time and energy, but a small passion that drives you is better than no passion at all. Small sparks give us confidence to light bolder fires.

Anita Roddick, who took The Body Shop from a passionate idea to more than 1,900 stores worldwide, says, "If you think you're too small to have an impact, try going to bed with a mosquito." Start with small sparks, and soon you will be rewarded with the blazing fire of bold passion.

6. *Translate your passions into written goals.* In the business world it's common knowledge that what gets measured gets done. A Harvard Business School study revealed that only 3 percent of the population have written goals, 14 percent have goals, just not written down, and 83 percent have no clearly

defined goals. The study further revealed that the 3 percent with written goals earned 10 times more than the others.

Individuals with written goals are more likely to have better health and happier marriages. The power of written goals is indisputable, and only after writing a goal down can you sincerely examine it and define the strategies to make it happen.

7. *Make time for your passions.* In a busy, demanding schedule, it's easy to believe we have no time for passions. If we believe that's so then we make it so. Conversely, if we believe in the promises we make to ourselves, then we will carve out the time to pursue a passion that promises fulfillment.

Many authors rise an hour early to finish writing a book. Many successful career women use their lunch hour to study, place important phone calls or otherwise make progress in pursuing their passions. Entrepreneurial homemakers stay up to pursue their venture long after the family has gone to bed.

Are you passionate about what you spend 60 to 80 percent of your time doing? If so, then you will undoubtedly succeed. If not, make it your mission to change that ratio. Live and work a passionate life. You deserve to be on fire.

8. *Align your relationships with your passions.* It's not uncommon for a woman's passion to conflict with important relationships. This is true whether the relationship is with your supervisor, your best friend or your life partner. Will you change your vision to hold on to the relationship or change the relationship to hold on to your passion?

An important success trait is the ability to detach from people who aren't on course with you. It doesn't mean that everyone you know and love has to agree totally with your life choices. But don't waste time with people who want to diminish you in any way.

I have a friend who put her career on hold after she married and had children. She stayed at home until the oldest was four years old, when she began doing volunteer work to get out of the house. That wasn't enough, so she took a full-time job, which required her to travel. She was making more money than her husband, even after four years off the market. Her in-laws, who believe a woman's only function is homemaker, bombarded her husband with their negative opinions. Emotionally torn, he wanted to support his wife but was conditioned by loyalty to his parents' ideals. Naturally, his wife also felt conflicted, eager to pursue her vision but emotionally invested in her husband and family.

I encouraged her to go with her vision, because it's her life. Too many women give up their career dreams to protect a relationship. That's traditional, but it can drive you into a mental institution. And some dreams, if you don't pursue them timely, will pass you by. When you're finally free to go after them, you've missed the window of opportunity. To her husband's credit, he went along because he valued the relationship as much as she did.

Conversely, a former student, whose husband felt threatened by her earning more money then he did, dissolved her successful consulting practice and gave up a six-figure income. To avoid conflict in her relationship she renounced her passion. Maybe she should have renounced her husband's limited thinking and surrounded herself instead with people who believed in her.

A relationship must be mutually beneficial, and any genuine relationship will adjust to change. When you recognize that a relationship is extinguishing your fire, ask yourself whether you should gracefully detach and move on. Communicate how much your vision means to you, do it in a relationship-friendly way, and the people in your life may surprise you.

Open a communication path to enroll in your vision the people who matter to you. The game of life is challenging enough when players support one another. And life is more fun when the people on your team are truly aligned in the direction your intuition says is right.

9. *Keep the passion alive by stoking the fire.* While enjoying a hobby or other activity, have you ever thought, "If I could do this every day I'd be happy"? Then you got your wish and discovered it wasn't enough. You didn't feel quite as ecstatic and alive as you had expected.

Not everyone can switch passions in midlife. You invest years in education, gaining experience and advancing in your profession. You build a support structure, and that structure depends on your continued involvement. Switching to a totally different profession means starting from ground level, reinvesting your resources in an unproven venture and climbing a different ladder to a different future. That's fine if you truly yearn to start over and your passion drives you in that new direction. Many people's passions burn brighter when they make sweeping changes.

At least once a week I'm ready to sell my company—or auction off my CEO position to the first bidder. I love my work and my company, but I don't love every aspect of it. Do you ever feel this way about your life, your job, your career? Stop and reevaluate. If you're like me, maybe you're not experiencing the dreaded "burnout" but only a need to stoke your fire.

Do what you do, but find a different focus. Or do what you do differently. My best growth ideas come when I toss out the old embers and stir things up.

Reinvent yourself, as Daryn Kagan did when she changed from news reporter to sportscaster. She shook up tradition and defied the odds, first by going after a position traditionally held by a man, then by using that leverage to vault ahead of the competition. Throughout those years, she followed her passion, which never had a chance to burn out because she kept stoking it.

What aspect of your passion have you not fully explored? What will set you ablaze? What new opportunities are available to you now? Passion is precious. Don't let the mundane routines that surface in any pursuit dampen your fire. Look within and find a spark you can fan to full flame again.

Ignite Your Fire with the
5 PROMISES

PROMISE 1
I Will Live and Work a Passionate Life

Write down at least one passion from the earlier exercises. Do it, even if it's only a spark.

_____

_____

_____

How do your passions relate to what you do now? Calculate the time you spend each day living and working your passions. If it's less than 75 percent, how can you increase that time?

_____

_____

_____

PROMISE 2
I Will Go for It or Reject It Outright

What holds you back from living your passions? Is it physical, mental, emotional or financial? Is it driven by adverse responsibilities or relationships? How can you eliminate or minimize the obstacles?

_____

_____

_____

*P*ROMISE 3

I Will Take One Action Step a Day Toward My Passionate Vision

What one action will you take today toward living your passions?

_____

_____

_____

*P*ROMISE 4

I Commit to Being a Success Student for Life

What do you need to know to pursue your passions? How can you obtain this knowledge? When will you commit to learning it?

_____

_____

_____

*P*ROMISE 5

I Believe as a Woman I Really Can Do Anything

Recall a passion that fired you up, however briefly. List three principles you can take from that to your next, bolder passion.

_____

_____

_____

Download the 5 Promises for Fire at InsideEveryWoman.com.

EVIE'S FIRE

Certain things that I'm on fire about push me forward, especially at work. Ever since I was young, I have always been passionate about making a person feel happy or pleased. In my first job, working as a cashier, this passion transcended into building good relationships with customers. Subsequently I was promoted to supervisor. Then I was promoted again, to a "cash clerk." I'm the last person who needs to be counting money, but my managers translated my passionate behavior to mean that I would probably do anything in that company well. Through passion for being a good employee and lots of recounting, I got through it.

Today, my passion is still customer service, and I have written and spoken professionally about the subject. Although my education is in marketing, I mentor and work directly with customers. I also train and coordinate customer service for a high-energy company, mentoring customer service representatives to be as passionate about our customers as I am.

No matter where you are in life, you have to be on fire about at least one aspect of your job to really make a difference and stand out. Passion is the one thing that gets me ahead. I'm still working on my college degree, but I've had no problem surpassing people who already have a college degree by making more money and holding higher positions. It doesn't make me more or less smart. My passion fuels my fire. I guess that says a lot about passion.

Evie, 35
Customer Relations Coordinator and
Marketing Creative

Women are born passionate and have the potential to live life passionately. Dig deep, discover the fire in your soul, then read on to see how intuitive vision can broaden your realm of possibilities.

Before I go out on the stage, I must place a motor in my soul.
When that begins to work, my legs and arms and my whole body
will move independently of my own will. But if I do not . . .
put the motor in my soul, I cannot dance.
—Isadora Duncan

The world always steps aside for people who know where they're going.
—Miriam Viola Larsen

See the change you want to be.
—Vickie L. Milazzo

INTUITIVE VISION

Imagine Unlimited Possibilities
to Capture Your Vision

Women and intuition go together like cats and curiosity. The concept that women are more in touch with instinctive inner guidance is so intrinsic to our culture that most people accept it without expecting any scientific explanation.

On the side of science, the larger splenium of the corpus callosum accounts for greater interconnectivity between the left and right hemispheres of women's cognitive brains. Some scientists believe this broader connection enables women to access both sides more quickly and more easily than men. Women are not more "right-brained," as is the myth; their brain functions are actually more holistic and generalized. We fluently engage the limbic brain, where higher emotions are stored, and the instinctive brain, which is responsible for self-preservation, and this holistic combination of emotion, instinct and cognition equates to women's intuition. Does it make sense to have such an extraordinary tool and not use it? Not in my book.

That's not to say that intuition is infallible. We can want passionately to go in a particular direction, and even have a clear vision of where we're going, only to be rerouted by circumstance. As an example, when I first realized that my nursing career was not taking me where I wanted to go, I imagined a new path. Since teaching was my lifelong passion, I envisioned a business teaching patients and their families how to improve their health, something hospitals had little interest in. A need for that service clearly existed, but there was no insurance reimbursement for patient education, so my heartfelt idea was not realistic. I imagined a passionate future only to hit a wall.

To satisfy my teaching passion, I taught a few classes at a senior citizen center, but that wouldn't pay the bills. Then I decided to become a legal nurse consultant, and was thrilled to realize I would be teaching attorneys and their clients about the healthcare issues in their cases. Rerouted and rekindled yet again, my passion burned even brighter when I began teaching other RNs to become legal nurse consultants.

Sometimes your vision doesn't materialize exactly as you imagine it, but trust it anyway. If you feel passionate enough, and continue to refocus your vision as needed, you'll find your true path. It's intuitive.

Intuitive vision is about connecting with your imagination, paying attention, trusting, perhaps experimenting a little, and seeing where that takes you. After I was in business for a number of years, the legal nurse consulting profession I created caught on and an association was formed. That association could not align with my vision to create a certification program. I felt so strongly that this was important for the industry's future that I created the program myself. Fired by my passion, trusting my intuitive vision and unwilling to accept a whole group's limitations, I created an entire curriculum, a certification credential and an even larger association. The National Alliance of Certified Legal Nurse Consultants remains the nation's largest legal nurse consulting association. I jumped off the accepted track, defined a new profession and its standards, and put my own train in motion.

My idea was fueled by a passionate vision. Sure, I had facts and experience to back me up, but not enough to convince a group that was afraid of change. Sure, their inability to see what I could see tested my beliefs, but my vision was so strong I had to go for it. After investing enormous amounts of time, money and energy in my program, I achieved staggering success, not only for myself but for thousands of other women who have graduated from my training program.

If anyone ever tells you one person can't accomplish anything big and shouldn't go against the odds, don't believe it. It worked for me. And it will work for you. It all starts with your intuitive vision.

ORDER OFF THE RIGHT MENU

My husband and I were having dinner with my dad at one of my favorite Italian restaurants. After an animated discussion with the waiter, my dad, always a picky eater, ordered a pasta dish that wasn't on the menu, telling the waiter exactly what he wanted in it.

The food came, beautifully presented and prepared exactly as requested. Bits of scallion, tomato, garlic and peppered chicken glistened over a bed of fettuccine, all infused with a light tomato-basil sauce and dusted with Parmesan cheese. My father's dish looked so good, I wanted his instead of my own.

I expected him to be delighted. Instead, he compared it to a different pasta dish from a different Italian restaurant. Rather than enjoying his dinner, he found fault with the waiter, the restaurant and the chef for not serving this other recipe. The dish was prepared wrong, he said, too many tomatoes, not enough garlic and the sauce wasn't right!

I sat stunned and amused. I reminded my dad that he had received exactly what he ordered. "I may have gotten what I ordered," Dad replied, "but it wasn't what I wanted."

Are you making your choices off the right menu? I see women every day who are living the wrong life, working the wrong career, because they ordered off the wrong menu. Haven't we all done that at times? We want different conditions in our career or relationships, but as long as we stay where we are, the changes we want are not even possible.

Do you feel cranky about your situation and environment? Are you exhausted by too many responsibilities and not enough time? If your life isn't where you want it to be, you may, like my father, have erroneous expectations.

As an employer, I love hiring young people, because I enjoy their enthusiasm and energy, but I prefer to get them after they've been seasoned by at least one other job experience. Otherwise, their expectations lean toward a naive vision of being an employee, and they become dissatisfied.

A lot of people get into a "perfect" marriage or career position only to find it's not what they thought they ordered. When making decisions that affect your life, check them against your passions and intuitive vision. If the dish you want is not on the menu, perhaps you're in the wrong place.

Equally important: Be open to ordering off new menus. If you find yourself in a situation that isn't exactly what you picture for your future, remain open to new experiences and you might find a new and greater passion. When I first began consulting with attorneys, I expected to work on legal cases involving my specialty, intensive care. But when an attorney handed me a case about a brain-injured baby, I discovered a new passion. By being open to new possibilities you will discover many unexpected passions. Life is an adventurous banquet filled with tasty and satisfying experiences. Feast occasionally at a brand-new restaurant.

SHOW UP WITH NO GUARANTEE

Intuitive vision doesn't mean blindly stepping off a cliff or dropping your paycheck on lottery tickets and trusting you'll win. Skydivers carefully pack their own parachutes, scuba divers check their own gear and entrepreneurs write business plans. When you start any new venture, you can and should strategize, but you can't guarantee the outcome. Skydivers break bones, scuba divers get the bends and businesses fail.

In life you have to trust in your intuitive vision enough to show up and invest the full effort with no guarantee of the upshot. That might feel scary, but the only thing certain is this: If you do nothing, you'll achieve nothing.

A fan once approached the great violinist Fritz Kreisler and commented, "I'd give my life to play as beautifully as you do." The violinist responded, "I did."

Showing up today, and paying the price today, determines tomorrow's success. If you want a guarantee, forget it. Trust your intuitive vision, make the investment and eventually the music will come.

When Kreisler began studying the violin, he had no assurance of playing at a local restaurant or at Carnegie Hall. He merely followed his intuitive vision. When I launched my legal nurse consulting certification program, I had no guarantee that anyone would show up, much less that the training program would attract thousands of nurses every year to this new profession of legal nurse consulting.

When you start any new venture you have no assurance it will be successful, satisfying or profitable. You have only your passion, whatever facts you've gathered and your intuitive vision.

SILENCE AROUSES IMAGINATION

Without even realizing it, we wake up daily to clutter pouring in—constant television or the Internet at home, talk radio in the car, TV news programs at the airport and loud music in restaurants. Soon our senses become dulled and our vision lusterless. How can a woman connect with her intuitive vision when she can't even think straight, constantly bombarded as she is with thousands of outside messages?

To conceive any vision you must first get quiet. Remove the clutter and turn down the volume. Consciously eliminate pervasive noise. Silence arouses imagination.

Make it your goal to eliminate clutter from your mind, your day and your life. I started with my physical environment, which is the easiest to control. I've successfully created an uncluttered house and an uncluttered office. Next I moved to uncluttering my mental environment. I'm still working on that one.

While I rarely watch TV or listen to talk radio, and I don't crave an hourly update on current events, I have my own clutter addiction to battle—movies. My addiction got so bad for a while that I found myself going to really bad movies, wondering later why I wasted that time and money. I still love going to good movies, but I must frequently recommit to not sitting in a movie theater just to get away from it all.

I appreciate that these activities are some of the most common ways to relax. But you cannot wake up to clutter, be bombarded with it all day and go to bed with that same level of intrusion and still have the mental space to find your intuitive vision. Choose renewing ways to relax, such as strolling through a park, soaking in the tub or reading a great book.

As with most ambitious endeavors, eliminating all the clutter in your life can seem overwhelming at first. The trick is to start small. Try these three easy steps:

1. *Clear your space.* Unclutter your physical environment at home and work. Take 10 minutes every day to file that stack of papers that's been sitting on your credenza for months. Devote 15 minutes a day to cleaning out a closet or room that's only slightly less attractive than the city dump. Don't tackle the whole attic. Start with one corner, then move on to another until it's done.

2. *Unclutter your mind.* Eliminate one outside stimulus, one TV show or one chatty phone call. Then eliminate another. Instead of reading three newspapers or magazines, read one. While driving, replace talk radio with inspirational CDs or music that stimulates ideas and opens a space for success. Meditate as you fall asleep or read something relaxing that brings you peace, not agitation.

Eliminate one recreation or hobby that no longer satisfies. Tom asked me recently, "Do you want to go to the art festival?" I used to enjoy this event, but that day it didn't appeal. I said, "No," and in that single word eliminated potential recreational clutter, opening that space for a more satisfying type of fun.

Be equally selective about how you spend time with friends and family. You might not think of a relationship as clutter, but it can be. Are casual, unsatisfying relationships keeping you from your vision? Would fewer, more meaningful relationships be more helpful? Assess whether a relationship is one that you value. If not, eliminate it or, at minimum, reduce the exposure. Don't succumb to guilt—especially where family is concerned. You don't have to like every family member, and you don't have to spend your annual vacation with them when a weekend will do. Uncluttering is about making choices in all the areas of your mind, space and time.

3. *Put off procrastination.* Procrastination leads to worry and anxiety, which is mind clutter. You're anxious about the up-coming meeting because the report due is still rough at best. You worry about overdrafting your bank account because you've put off balancing your checkbook. Instead, just put off procrastination.

Eliminate one area of procrastination each week. Schedule it in your calendar, as you would any important appointment, and when that time arrives, do what needs to be done. Your mind will feel refreshingly alert and uncluttered.

Yet procrastination is not always bad. I hear people say "finish what you start" or "you had that idea, where did you go with it?" Every day I wake up with new ideas, but there is only so much time, and selective procrastination allows the best ideas to rise to the top. Misplaced stubbornness, as in "I started it, I have to finish it," can exhaust you as you plow onward in the wrong direction.

Intuitive vision keeps you focused. In the emergency room all nurses learn the value and skill of triage. When several patients come in at once, nurses treat the sickest ones first. That's triage.

You can triage ideas. All ideas are not equal, so match your ideas to your intuitive vision to determine which to develop first.

Selective procrastination also eliminates unnecessary busyness. Imagine a low-priority task, perhaps starting a routine project or writing a letter. You procrastinate, and at the end of the day or the week that situation resolves itself. The project is canceled or the topic of the letter gets resolved with a two-minute phone call. Selective procrastination, or triage, combined with your intuitive vision can eliminate the clutter of unnecessary tasks.

TRUST YOUR WAY THROUGH THE CHAOS

Every nurse has known patients who lived when they should have died and patients who died when they should have lived. What made the difference? A nurse will say it's all about what's going on upstairs, the powerful mind-body connection. Many health obstacles are mental. The mind-success connection is equally strong, and many obstacles to our success are also mental. Your intuitive vision enables you to bypass such obstacles. Some women rely more on facts, while others rely more on feelings. There is no "right way" to be, but we all have the inborn perception to "feel" our way successfully along an unlighted path.

I learned this when I was stuck on a curb in Ho Chi Minh City, which residents still call Saigon. My objective, a restaurant where my husband and lunch awaited me, stood on the opposite side of the street. I could see the food and smell it, and I had built up quite an appetite. Crossing the street sounds like a simple task, but my objective might as well have been the far side of the moon. Tu Do Street was crammed with motor scooters, bicycles, cyclos (pedaled rickshaws), cars, trucks and buses. The fewer wheels on a contraption, the more passengers it seemed to carry.

Even the center lines contributed to the confusion. Rather than dividing the traffic into two lanes, each moving in opposite directions, the yellow lane markers apparently served only to indicate that you were on a paved road. People passed, stopped, turned around and crisscrossed center lines with utter abandon. Traffic flowed both ways in the same lane, more traffic merged from side streets and even more people pushed their scooters off the curbs into the flow. Traffic bore down on me from front, back, sides and all angles. It was an incredible chaos.

Even when the signal light turned red, traffic continued to flow as drivers blatantly ignored the signal. Vehicles waiting at the green light would slowly edge forward into the traffic, eventually building up enough momentum to stop the crossing vehicles from running the red light. Traffic then flowed correctly until the light changed and the whole process started again.

Above this onslaught the flashing "walk" sign serenely taunted me from the far side of the street. I was ready to abandon lunch with Tom and look for a baggie of lemonade and a roasted lizard on a stick when a mature Vietnamese gentleman took my arm.

In English, he kindly said, "Crossing the street is not a problem, but a dance." With that we stepped off the curb and into the maelstrom. My heart pounded as we walked slowly across. Instead of greeting us with blaring horns, irate shouts and screeching brakes, drivers saw and adjusted to us. As long as we made no sudden movements (like diving for the curb), we were fine. I felt as if we were gracefully swimming through a school of fish. The tempest flowed smoothly around us, in all directions, and before I knew it we were across.

Learning to dance through the chaos of Saigon's traffic is much like learning to follow your intuitive vision. It's a combination of intention, timing and trust. Do you dance gracefully through the chaos of your life and career? Do you struggle against it, exhausting yourself and colliding with others? Or do you detour, avoiding possible collisions altogether?

Develop your intuitive vision and learn to trust it. Certainly, collisions and accidents will happen. Even when things are going well, a big truck may hurtle out of the blue, forcing you to stop or change directions or maybe running you over. But guided by instinct, emotion and cognition, you can dance your way through this chaos and find the lighted path.

IMAGINATION TRUMPS KNOWLEDGE

When we think of vision, geniuses spring to mind. Topping the list are Leonardo da Vinci and Albert Einstein.

Da Vinci imagined many inventions that were made possible only after technology caught up with his vision. He was 40 years ahead of Copernicus when he wrote, "The sun does not move." To study the stars, Da Vinci imagined "a large magnifying lens." Sixty years later Galileo made it happen. Da Vinci also envisioned parachutes, armored tanks and helicopters, often including detailed drawings in his notes. This one person's imagination was more advanced than an entire world's knowledge.

Albert Einstein's thoughts took simple form, but with far-reaching possibilities. He tried to imagine what a light beam would look like if he were to race alongside it. "Imagination," he wrote, "is more important than knowledge." Eventually, his mental images led him to form his world-changing theory of relativity. Years later science finally proved what Einstein had theorized based on his studies and intuitive vision.

A female genius you may not know was Margaret Knight. Mattie's talent for invention emerged when, like many children of the 1860s, she worked in a cotton mill. After witnessing a mill accident at age 12, she envisioned and designed a shuttle-restraining

device to prevent workers from being injured. Later she envisioned
a paper bag to replace the tall envelopes being used to hold groceries and other purchases. At 29, she invented a machine part that
would automatically fold and glue the flat-bottom bags we use
today. Dubbed "the female Edison," Mattie eventually patented 26
other inventions, including rotary engines and automatic tools.

Despite the "fact" that many important discoveries resulted
from intuitive vision, rigidly left-brained, fact-focused thinkers
often dismiss intuition as useless. Don't let them intimidate you.
Women need to tap into their intuitive intelligence. Even fact-
focused "experts" often disagree about which facts to rely on, as
well as the interpretation of so-called facts. Every set of facts is
subject to as many interpretations as there are interpreters. If you
wait for facts to weigh in with your vision, you might be waiting
long after someone has grabbed the vision and run with it.

J. K. Rowling's imagination defied all the facts. The facts were
emphatic: Children today don't read, and even if they did read,
Rowling's book was too long, too dark and much too complex.
Rowling's passionate vision told her that children would indeed
read her book. In any case, her passion compelled her to write it.
Despite the rejection of her first book by numerous editors and
publishing houses, her Harry Potter series has enraptured children
and adults everywhere with its imaginative plots and vivid charac-
ters. Rowling became the first author to become a billionaire from
the sale of her "unreadable" books.

Artist Barbara Hepworth, one of the three major British
sculptors of the early 20th century, also defied the facts. She had
a vision of stone that transcended the solid mass other sculptors saw. "Stone is too solid. It needs to be more transparent,"
Hepworth told her peers. Because of her vision she demanded
more from her sculpture than was traditional. She sought to
incorporate open space into the solidity of the closed form. In

1931, Hepworth became the first sculptor to pierce the stone for abstract effect. Her creations began with geometric and organic shapes, which she hollowed out and then filled with stringed configurations. Her vision brought to the world an art form previously unknown.

Our intuitive vision is uniquely intelligent, bigger and more powerful than any set of facts. If imagination was good enough for Da Vinci, Einstein, Knight, Rowling and Hepworth, it's good enough for me.

Our emotional brain, the limbic region where passions and fears battle each other, cannot distinguish between reality and intuitive vision, and our rational, thinking brain, the cortex, cannot feel those emotional battles. Since the limbic brain cannot think but only feel, it reacts to your dreams as it would to a real experience. Knowing this, you can impassion your mind with any desire you actively envision, and that passion will in turn drive your positive actions toward making the vision a reality. In other words, if you vividly envision the desired result and reinforce that desire by frequently revisiting the vision, your passion will make it happen.

Practice Mentally Everything You Want to Accomplish

To become successful, you must first see yourself as successful. Visualize the process of attainment. This practice is commonplace in sports and the performing arts. Great performers such as Alicia Alonso and most great athletes practice in their heads even more than they do in the physical world. A basketball player mentally throws thousands of baskets, dancers mentally dance thousands of steps. This mental practice is as important to success as actual time spent playing or dancing. Even a racecar driver prepares by visualizing herself making laps around the track on which she's about to race.

When I have a new keynote speech to deliver I mentally practice that speech 5 or 10 times for every chance I have to rehearse
it aloud. Without that mental "warm-up," my rehearsals would be
exhausting.

Envision your success over and over again—approaching,
taking action, succeeding—playing a melody on your favorite
instrument, getting that promotion, building a table or a flourish-
ing business. You must see the change you want to be and where
you want to go. It doesn't matter if nobody else sees it.

Imagine Your New Future

Envision a future improved by your actions. Vividly see the benefits you'll receive and the people who will enjoy the fruits of your
efforts.

Limber up your imagination with this lifestyle exercise:

1. Allow a passionate desire to surface. Perhaps it's a new home,
   car or office. Or maybe it's a tropical island you've always
   wanted to visit.

2. Envision yourself within that lifestyle, relaxing in that fabulous home, driving the car or walking that tropical beach.
   Enhance your vision with all the sensory details you can em-
   bed—sounds, smells, colors, textures, tastes. Make it real.

3. Revisit this enhanced vision until it springs instantly to mind
   anytime you think of your future.

If you desire this result deeply enough to hold it firm in your
imagination as you work toward it, then a month, a year or several years from now, you will make this vision a reality.

Even if you don't believe visualizing works, even if you believe
only geniuses like Einstein and performers like Alicia Alonso have

such powerful imaginations, or you think it's too "out there" to be useful in everyday life, try it anyway. It's totally free and there are no harmful side effects.

ACCELERATE ACHIEVEMENT WITH HYPNAGOGIC IMAGERY

Testing experts tell us that to better retain information we truly want to learn, we should study it 30 minutes before bedtime. Our mind absorbs the information better when at rest.

How many times have you said, "I need to sleep on that"? While you may have meant that remark as a figure of speech, it actually helps to let your subconscious mind work on ideas, problems and decisions independently of your conscious mind.

Another area of time and space you might find particularly useful is that state of intermediate consciousness immediately preceding or following sleep. It's a fertile ground for imagination.

To germinate ideas, envision a desired result as you are falling asleep. Incorporate images, sounds, smells, textures, whatever comes to mind, but avoid "thinking," that is, trying to impose logic. This will only keep you awake. Simply let your mind drift off after envisioning what you want to have happen. When you awaken, recapture that vision, along with any fluttering ideas that accompany it. As quickly as possible, write down your thoughts for your conscious mind to ponder later.

I know a writer who plotted a short story using hypnagogic imagery. Her visions were so distinct and rapid, they kept waking her. To avoid losing them, she grabbed an envelope and jotted down her thoughts, then lay back down to sleep. Minutes later, she woke again, envisioning the next twist. That went on for nearly an hour. The next morning, her envelope was filled with scribbles, mere threads of ideas, but salient threads, which she quickly developed into a prize-winning story.

Why not put this powerful process to work for you? Try hypnagogic imagery tonight. You will be astonished at the outcome.

HITCH YOUR VISION TO YOUR PASSION

When your intuitive vision and your passion are richly connected, your decisions will lead you quickly to success. Connect your passion to your intuitive vision in three ways:

1. *Create an environment for success.* Match your vision to something you're good at. I took dance lessons after finishing college, and I think it would be cool to be a dancer. But I'm just not that talented on my feet. I had to match my vision to what I could actually do. I could be passionate about dancing, but taking it to a professional level never would have happened. Time and energy wasted.

   When your intuitive vision matches your personal strengths, then you must believe in it. If you believe it can happen, you're more likely to create an environment in which it can happen and to take the necessary action to make it happen.

2. *Give every success an encore.* As you venture into new success, don't forget your past successes and all you learned from them. Success promotes success. The more you succeed, the more you will succeed.

   When your intuitive vision challenges you to grow or change, give your past successes an encore. Anytime you need a shot of courage, relive the applause and the good decisions. Get the visceral boost you need, then apply what you learned to your new vision. New challenges put you back in the limelight, and that place can be scary, but every time you encore a small success, the applause sets you on fire and the next success comes easier.

3. ***Don't labor over decisions.*** Passionate women who trust their intuitive vision are quick and decisive. They tell themselves, "I'm going for it. If it doesn't work out, I'll adjust." Gather the facts, consider your options, then go with what feels right.

Often it doesn't matter what you do as long as you do something. You'll never have a guaranteed outcome, but if you don't make the decision, you'll have a result anyway. It's more exhilarating to activate the result, and perhaps take a few falls, than to waver and do nothing for fear of the wrong result. In being a mother, for example, how do you ever know how to do it exactly right? Yet not knowing all the answers doesn't keep a woman from having children. She trusts her instincts for that child's future.

Some of my students will take four months creating promotional brochures, striving to make them perfect, when a better choice would be to move forward, make the sales calls and perfect the materials as they go. Once they snag their first client, students always express regret about taking so long to get moving.

Avoid analysis paralysis. Take an action step. If it leads you into uncharted territory, you can always change the route. But at least now you're moving.

BE READY WITH YOUR NEXT VISION

My writer friend spent several years accomplishing the big goal of becoming a published author. She followed her intuitive vision and attributes her success to staying focused, believing in the vision, rehearsing mentally what she wanted to achieve physically, and even using hypnagogic imagery to make it happen. When success came, she celebrated and jumped into the new lifestyle with both feet running. She became so caught up in her success that when the glory and excitement waned, she realized she had no vision of what came next. And what happened? Nothing came next. Yes, she published more novels, but she no longer had an audacious goal pulling at her. Her career leveled off, then began a downward slide. To start the process over again, she retrieved her deepest-held passions and summoned a new intuitive vision of her literary future. Now she continues to renew and extend her visions, anticipating success to follow success.

What's the next success you want to achieve? Success is a journey. Always assume more success will come, and be ready with your next vision.

Capture Your Intuitive Vision with the

5 PROMISES

PROMISE 1

I Will Live and Work a Passionate Life

Begin each day imagining in detail the place where your passionate vision will lead you. Describe that vision here.

PROMISE 2

I Will Go for It or Reject It Outright

Write down five areas in your life you will unclutter to make time and space for living your passionate vision.

PROMISE 3

I Will Take One Action Step a Day Toward My Passionate Vision

Assess where you are in reaching your passionate vision. Imagine taking the next step. Describe what you see.

----

*P*ROMISE 4
I Commit to Being a Success Student for Life

List three times you trusted your intuition and really went for it. What did you learn from those experiences? What signs told you that your intuition was or was not on track?

_____

_____

_____

*P*ROMISE 5
I Believe as a Woman I Really Can Do Anything

Write down one success that came from trusting your intuitive vision.

_____

_____

_____

From that success create three affirming statements about yourself. Connect each one to a daily activity—showering, applying makeup. Declare your affirmations every time you engage in that activity.

_____

_____

_____

Download the 5 Promises for Intuitive Vision at InsideEveryWoman.com.

MAGGIE'S *Vision*

Since I was a small girl I always had a plan, and I knew I would follow my life on my own terms. I imagined from the beginning what I wanted—a simple, fulfilling life surrounded by art and beauty. Obviously, my imagination drew the path and set the milestones for every step of the way: where I wanted to be, how fast I wanted to get there and what I was willing to sacrifice.

Early on I knew that I wanted to be an entrepreneur. I started drawing a map, a plan. I understood that surrounding myself with people who had integrity, intelligence and focus would help support my goals. I made a personal commitment to learn everything I could about achieving success at every level of my life.

I started with architecture as the main focus of my career. I tried to expose myself to significant architectural and design work, to help feed my passion and gain inspiration.

As it turned out, today I'm not an architect but a graphic designer. I'm not leading a team of architects or construction workers but a design team, which gives me other avenues to explore in expressing my vision and helping my clients.

I come from a culture where the highest-level positions and professional respect are reserved for men. My vision was not to be limited by that reality but to exceed every expectation. That is not to say it has been easy—I have always had to work especially hard to prove myself academically or in the workplace. I am the first woman in my family to pursue a professional career. I set out to excel as a designer, problem solver and entrepreneur while balancing my responsibilities as a daughter, sister, friend, wife and mother.

I've always had a hunger to grow as a person and to learn more from others. I have sought out role models for every aspect of my life. I try to understand what these people have done and apply their wisdom to my intuitive vision. I want to get there faster, stronger and better.

*M*AGGIE, 33
Co-Owner, Graphic Design Firm

Now that you know how awesome you can be when you capture your intuitive vision, let's explore the role engagement plays in achieving your desired future.

Far away there in the sunshine are my highest aspirations.
I may not reach them, but I can look up and see their beauty,
believe in them and try to follow where they lead.
—Louisa May Alcott

If you want something done, ask a woman.
—Margaret Thatcher

What you engage and focus on
is where you will yield results.
—Vickie L. Milazzo

ENGAGEMENT

Engage Commitment to Achieve Big Things

Women are tycoons of commitment, a sight to behold and a force
to be reckoned with. The average woman has more complex responsibilities than the crew of NASA's mission control, and we
handle every one of them. Forget Superman, Spiderman and
Batman. I'll take Wonder-Working Woman any time. By nature,
women are giving and nurturing, ready to engage the Devil himself
when loved ones are at risk. And this natural edge is a mighty force
when we engage any challenge. Because we are tenaciously faithful
to the commitments we undertake, anything is possible.

But not just any commitment will do. Women who commit
to a passionate vision reach the highest levels of success.

Society is complex, with family, friends, career, and spiritual and social obligations. Your opportunities are boundless.
Women can handle a lot, and if we're not careful we find our-

selves doggedly committing our energy to every person or situation that demands our time. Before long we have no energy left. Don't become a victim of "one day, some day, I'll get around to living my dreams, and in the meantime I'll help everyone else live theirs."

Similarly, we can be so overcommitted in one area of obligation that we overlook other important parts of our vision. In the early days of my business I kept my mind and hands busily engaged with every detail. Even after hiring employees, I tried to handle my own work and still oversee the details of theirs. Overcommitment robbed me of important social events with family and friends—birthdays, weddings, even my stepmother's funeral—but business boomed.

Engagement starts with choice. Choose the objective of your engagement with your passionate vision in mind. As a CEO, I encourage my staff to engage fully on a big project, to put their phone to voice mail and close their e-mail. Sometimes they encourage my engagement by covering my desk with projects that "need" my immediate involvement. At those times I joke that CEO means "Controlled Entirely by Others," smile, slide their stack to the back credenza and get back on focus.

By briefly revisiting your passionate vision, you can narrow down commitments, eliminate or delegate anything that will take you off focus and free up time to pursue your passions.

At age 16, Danica Patrick narrowed her focus and engaged her vision for automobile racing, a field traditionally dominated by men. She dreamed of competing in the Indianapolis 500. To gain the necessary experience, she left her Illinois home and family for England and spent four years honing her driving skills, racing day in and day out. At 23, she competed in her first Indianapolis 500 and finished an unprecedented fourth. Focused engagement guaranteed her success.

Passionately believing in the path you're on helps you narrow your commitments. By making judicious choices, you engage your day, your week and all the minutes that make up your life in pursuit of commitments that reflect the fire of your vision.

DITCH PERFECTIONISM

Step out, try new things and expect to make mistakes. When your best efforts go south, look upon these mistakes as tools for growth. If you never tried anything new, you would certainly make fewer mistakes, but would you ever accomplish anything worth remembering?

If 50 percent of your ideas succeed, you're better than the average baseball player, who generally bats around .264, less than a one-in-three success rate. Sheryl Swoopes, three-time Olympic gold medalist and two-time WNBA Most Valuable Player, doesn't sink every shot. Opera soprano Erika Miklosa occasionally sings off key. And even award-winning pastry chef Sherry Yard has a soufflé that falls. When you study successful people, you'll find that most of them achieved success through the mistakes they made along the way. Embrace the value and power of making mistakes.

When I made the ultimate commitment to get married, one of my best friends, Beth, who shares my perfectionist tendencies, told me, "Vickie, your wedding day will not be perfect. Something will go wrong. Don't let it get in the way of enjoying your special day."

She was way off. Not just one wrong thing happened, but lots. Our favorite minister was out of town and the replacement minister announced the wrong guest speaker. We arranged the reception on the top floor of a downtown skyscraper, where my stepmother, who was afraid of elevators, wouldn't go. I realized it was a bad idea to invite my ex-fiancé when he stole a piece of my underwear and wore it on his head like a hat during the reception. Not even a pair from Victoria's Secret, but my stretched-out cotton briefs—the kind you wear after the honeymoon.

Today those imperfections are fun memories. How often have you let minor screw-ups rob you of the enjoyment of an experience? Think back to a situation that went so wrong you wanted to scream, cry, kick the wall or even kick yourself. Is that outcome so important to you today? Can you remember where things started to slide into failure? Or who was at fault? Time and distance are wonderful at devolving moments of great calamity into insignificance. If you can detach emotionally to view a situation, you can laugh at it and learn from it. Nothing in life is ever perfect. When we demand perfection, we're bound to be frustrated.

In her first Indianapolis 500, Danica Patrick spun her race car into the wall. She later stalled during a pit stop, which dropped her to 16th place, and nearly ran out of fuel with six laps to go. Still she managed to finish fourth.

Mistakes are perfect experiences to learn from. Ditch perfectionism! Lighten up! Frequently the best ideas and opportunities come from the mistakes we make. None of us gets through life without making mistakes, but a lot of people miss out on life trying to avoid them. You can't win a race if you don't get on the track.

As an example, after presenting successful one-day seminars, I decided to expand the seminars to three days. I booked hotels nationwide, revised the curriculum and invested in promotion, but I failed to get a profitable response.

Panic might have led to canceling the whole idea. Instead, I restrategized and expanded the seminar to six days with certification. I tripled the price and mailed out new promotional brochures, and the new strategy exploded into success. Without the mistake of trying a three-day seminar, would I ever have stepped up to the six-day certification program that is now the bedrock of my entire business? Ditch perfectionism and you'll find it much easier to engage your passions.

ENGAGE YOUR FEARS TO CONQUER THEM

Lady Jessica in Frank Herbert's novel *Dune* taught her son, "Fear is the mind killer." Fear is also the enemy of engagement. Even when we're passionately committed to an idea or a goal, fear can stop us cold. Fear comes in many guises—fear of failure, fear of success, fear of looking silly. Conquering fear in one area boosts courage in other areas.

As I've mentioned, I get panicky at cliff-hanging heights, and I never really saw the point in skydiving. I don't fear heights in general, but I'm terrified of dangling on a high ledge. For years I vowed to never step out of an airplane unless I could plant my two feet firmly on an air-conditioned jetway. Then one Saturday I stepped out of an open airplane door at 14,000 feet.

The only time I'd tasted air near that altitude was standing solidly in the shadow of Mount Everest, and I had hiked to that altitude. Nevertheless, when two fearless, thrill-seeking women from my company decided to skydive, I chose to engage my fear of heights and join them (and drag Tom along, too).

Living a passionate life is a lot like skydiving. You have to engage commitment and step out into a boundless and unpredictable future if you want to fly high. This is the joy of life—when no matter the outcome, you still step out.

Acknowledging fear is your first step in conquering it. What is the worst that could happen?

In skydiving, terrible things can happen, including quadriple-gia or death. Mine was no fabricated fear. The week I was to jump I learned from one of my students that her paraplegia resulted from a skydiving accident. All my fears crowded back to waylay my commitment.

Although I was terrified, I jumped anyway. The 60-second free fall at 120 miles per hour was both scary and exhilarat-ing—and instantaneously the longest and shortest minute of my life. I would do it all over again for the delicious high of conquer-ing fear. Who knows what great accomplishments that fear had undermined over the years?

Fear can also commit you to the wrong people, wrong ideal or wrong decision. You participate in office gossip because you're afraid of being left out. You reluctantly commit to the car pool and miss an important work deadline. I once put off severing a business relationship with a subcontractor longer than I should have, wor-rying about replacing her. What if I couldn't find a replacement? What if a big project blew in and I couldn't finish it on time?

The best cure for fear is action. Think it through, decide what feels right, then do it. As Pat Schroeder said, "You can't wring your hands and roll up your sleeves at the same time."

Uncertainty is the sister of fear, and adequate preparation banishes uncertainty. In jumping out of that airplane, I had one audacious goal—to step out. Being pushed out didn't qualify.

A prerequisite video, guaranteed to scare off anyone easily intimidated, contained no fewer than five warnings about serious injury or death. A 10-page waiver was artfully drafted to scare the crap out of anyone who actually read it before signing. But my Zen-like tandem master, Scott, who had made 4,500 jumps, in-stantly put me at ease. If I was to entrust my life to anyone, surely Scott was the right choice.

The best advice Scott gave me was, "You don't have to be perfect. Your only goal today is to have fun." Beyond my commitment of stepping out—and having fun—I wasn't concerned about anything—well, other than dying.

Rally a Support Team

Even a veteran skydiver never jumps without a pilot to fly her to altitude and a certified rigger to pack her reserve chute. Like skydivers, smart women engage risk when backed by a trusted support team. Your team cheers you on, holds you accountable and provides a lifeline, ensuring that you will live through the experience to engage the next risk.

Scott boosted my confidence further when he shared that one of his clients had skydived for the first time on her 85th birthday and joyfully awaits her birthday dive every year. His reassurance vanquished a discouraging message I had received from one of my staff who came to watch. Immediately before we climbed into the airplane, she said, "I can't believe you're really doing this." When I playfully reminded her that I thought she'd come to encourage me, she said, "I'm here to talk you out of it."

Knowing she was expressing her fear from a place of love and concern, I appreciated that she cared, but I chose to discard her message. I had to face my fear.

Step Out to Fly High

The ride up to altitude was dreadfully slow. When we leveled off at 14,000 feet and they opened the side door of the airplane, the magnitude of my engagement became very real, very quickly. I pulled on my helmet and goggles. Scott snapped my harness securely to his. Suddenly, Tom and the jumpers before me were gone, and Scott moved us toward the open door. I remembered the instructor saying, "Once you're in the plane, 'No, No, No' means 'Go, Go, Go.'" Not looking down, not thinking about what I was doing, and still fully conscious, I stepped out.

At 6,000 feet, my 60-second free fall was over and my parachute opened. The pace of the experience instantly changed from frenetic overdrive to stillness and quiet. A mile above the earth, the sinking sun had never looked more beautiful. Minutes later, my feet hit familiar ground. I landed almost gracefully, exhilarated, knowing I had engaged my fear of heights and conquered it.

This monumental accomplishment raised the bar for me. If I could step out at 14,000 feet, I could do anything on the ground. To fly high, you'll have to step out into a boundless and unpredictable future, but at the end of the day, an engaged life is a more satisfying life.

BREAK THE "FEEL-GOOD" ADDICTION

How does a busy woman cope with the mounting demands and pressures of achieving her passionate vision while all around her life intrudes? In today's world, you're constantly sabotaged by nonproductive energy wasters that do nothing substantial for your future success. Because we like to feel good, many of us are addicted to majoring in minor accomplishments—answering e-mail, straightening, organizing and reorganizing. By majoring in minor things we never get to our big commitments.

Breaking the "feel-good" addiction opens the door to achievement. As I write this chapter, my freezer at home is on the fritz. I'm tempted to call and nudge the repairman, which won't make him arrive one minute sooner, but would make me feel good—until I realize it's diverting me from writing.

The feel-good addiction is insidious for those of us who like to check things off because you feel briefly elated after completing each small task. In the long term this cheap high is guaranteed to frustrate, overwhelm and stress. You'll start questioning how you can be so busy yet accomplish so little of importance.

The feel-good addiction begins with the way you start your day. "I'll knock this out quickly and strike it off my checklist." Or "I can't look at that stack of trivia in my in-box without going after it."

Is this feel-good start to your day the best use of your time? You'll be tempted to deal immediately with each issue. After all, it only takes two minutes to fire off an e-mail or three minutes to scan a publication for useful articles. Since you're not yet feeling the day's time constraints, these trivia steal more attention than they deserve. Two minutes turns into 20 as one item leads to another. Before you know it, quitting time arrives and you haven't accomplished one thing toward your passionate vision.

Even if you set them aside, these small tasks buzz around in your head and distract you for the rest of the day. A colleague misquoted you in an e-mail to your boss, or you need to locate receipts for your expense report. Although you defer action until 4:00 p.m., the issue agitates you all day. Don't let that happen. Distraction diffuses your focus on important matters. Put small tasks out of sight and out of mind until the designated time to deal with them.

What you engage and focus on is where you will yield results. Trivia saps the creative energy you need for accomplishing your audacious goals. When you stop engaging the fire of your passionate vision, you lose desire and motivation. You start to believe you're not cut out to achieve the future you've imagined.

ENGAGE ONE BIG THING AT A TIME

Engaging Big Things guarantees worthwhile achievement comparable to skydiving. You'll become addicted to momentum—a far more lasting high than the transitory feel-good of checking off trivial tasks. Identify three Big Things that connect to your passionate vision, then choose one to schedule your day around. Start strong and you'll experience genuine elation from achieving real goals and solving real problems.

Once you're engaged in accomplishing Big Things, you'll approach routine matters with laser-sharp focus, quickly deleting, delegating and experiencing fewer distractions.

More important, your creativity and productivity catch fire and the momentum keeps you pumped. You'll glide through your day full of confidence and satisfaction from achieving significant milestones.

Engage Momentum in Eight Easy Steps

1. *Define three Big Things.* Your vision might be to get promoted, live on the ocean or achieve financial security. A Big Thing might be to take on a high-profile work project, locate and buy a property or develop a household budget. Set a target date for completing your three Big Things.

2. *Challenge your engagement.* Ask: "Am I really going for it?" or "If it's too tough will I quit?" Make sure it's the right engagement for you at this time.

3. *Set aside sacred "momentum time."* First thing each week, schedule a substantial chunk of uninterrupted time (aim for two hours) for projects that support at least one of your Big Things. To carve out time, attach a time increment to your daily tasks, no matter how small. Examine every activity and

decide how to eliminate it, delegate it, hire it out or do it faster.

If part of your day is rarely interrupted (such as early morning or late evening), reserve it for momentum time. My favorite is early morning before my office opens, when I can knock out Big Things three times faster. You'll finish that huge report that seemed impossible or wrestle that new training program into comprehension.

Keep your momentum time sacred. Use phrases such as "I'll be available in one hour. What time after that works best for you?"

You can relegate personal goals to weekends, but don't assume that's necessary. I awake at 4:00 a.m. to carve time for myself. Maybe your best time is evenings, after your children are down for the night. Or maybe you can claim two evenings a week when your family fends for themselves for supper.

If one of your Big Things is work related, start your day with a two-hour uninterrupted chunk, then gradually add more two-hour momentum sessions each day.

4. *Let nothing stop you.* Set a start time and stick to it. You lose momentum "warming up your engine" with busywork. Banish all thoughts and interruptions that don't relate to your Big Thing. Put your phone on voice mail and don't open your e-mail or worry about your ill family member. Worry is a useless emotion. You can do it all later.

Develop a ritual to cleanse your mind—music, a cup of tea, an affirmation. A cluttered or tense mind accomplishes little.

If you get distracted, even briefly, commit to stopping the distraction. While writing this chapter, I caught myself firing off an e-mail to my marketing director. I stopped and jotted a note to handle it later. I always have paper handy for those sudden bursts—whether of brilliance or distraction. Don't let even the smallest energy waster slip in. Minutes add up to hours, hours to days.

A decade of poor work habits won't change overnight. As with exercise, what's difficult at first becomes easy. The more progress you see, the more addicted you'll become to momentum.

5. *Alternate momentum time with "weed pulling."* Miscellaneous routine tasks are like weeds—no matter how often you get rid of them, they never go away. Yet they do have to be handled, and pulling a few weeds can provide a break from more intensive work. Categorize tasks into Big Things or weeds. After each momentum session, devote 30 minutes to weed pulling—handling mail, phone calls or other minor chores.

Clump several small tasks. If you sequentially open mail, pay bills, file the receipts and drop the outgoing mail into a basket, you're being efficient. Never handle any communication (paper or e-mail) more than once, if possible.

Don't try to tackle all your weeds at once. Prioritize. Set aside one day periodically to do the deep weeding and organizing. Deep cleaning is cathartic.

If you need a five-minute break from your Big Thing, don't tackle the weeds. They will only distract. Use those five minutes to refresh your energy for your Big Thing with a stretch or bit of nourishment.

Finally, don't get addicted to pulling weeds. Occasionally substitute a more leisurely lunch or 30 minutes of reading.

6. *Focus on one Big Thing at a time.* When you engage in too much at once, you risk finishing nothing. Finish your first Big

Thing or at least reach a significant milestone before embarking on the next. I have difficulty following my own advice on this, but I remind myself to focus.

7. *Let go of bad ideas.* When my company decided to update our training curriculums for our home-study program and six-day seminar, we put extensive time into writing the material. It was almost completed when we realized we were creating a monster. The two programs were alike in content but totally different in presentation, which meant that every time we changed a page we'd have to rewrite and reprint both packages. It still breaks my heart to think of the hours that went into this revision before we wised up and created one curriculum that works for both.

   That's an example of a "great" idea that wasn't so great after all. No matter how much it hurt, we had to let it go. It's okay to let go of a bad idea.

8. *Safeguard your momentum.* Accept that you won't please everyone. Someone is bound to be unhappy about the changes you make to focus on your Big Things. They'll get over it. Stop feeling guilty and stay true to your goals. Surround yourself with friends, family and peers who support your vision. Discard all discouraging messages. This is your engagement, not anyone else's.

The more you do, the more you'll do! Engage momentum and jump out there.

ENGAGE IN WHAT'S RIGHT, NOT WHAT'S EASY

Despite your belief in the path you've chosen, not everything you engage will come easy. Your teenage daughter's recital falls on the same evening as your company gala. The software you desperately need to understand totally boggles your mind.

I'm committed to my business, which includes substantial travel and spending long days at the office. I'm also committed to special relationships with family and friends. Calling my dad every day is not always easy because of my schedule, but it feels right to do that. Our conversations are often brief, but wherever I am, I make the call.

My company is small, about 25 employees plus a number of independent contractors. Working as closely as we do, it's impossible not to develop friendships; in fact, I prefer working with competent people whom I also like. But this makes being a boss particularly tough when employee issues arise. The first time I had to fire an employee, I agonized over it. For support and advice I called my friend, Mary Ann, a successful business owner. She said, "Vickie, you know you have to do it. I promise that one day you won't even remember that person's name. Just do it."

It sounds harsh now, but the way she phrased it got through to me. No matter how much I dreaded firing a person I'd grown to care about, it was the right thing. The next day I terminated her. That night, in bed with Tom and a glass of wine, I cried and laughed about how tough it was, but it was done. The nudge from my friend helped me do what was right, not what was easy.

ENGAGE THE DETAILS

In coaching women for 24 years, I've observed that for many the vision is the easy part. Committing to the details that convert the vision into reality is tough. How many good ideas never get off the drawing board? Success doesn't ride in on a magic carpet, even when fueled by passionate vision. Success is ultimately about implementing uncountable details.

If your vision includes living in an Italian villa, you might engage in learning Italian at a language school in Florence, where you experience the culture while you learn. Fun! The success comes not from eating pasta every day in Italian trattorias, but from tedious language lessons every day for 12 weeks.

So often I'll hear someone ask, "Why is that woman successful? I'm just as talented, skilled and inventive as she is, so why not me?" The successful woman has engaged in the details that collectively complete her passionate vision. If your vision is a painting, engagement lies in taking action, applying paint to canvas. The details are the tiny brush strokes of paint that complete the picture and make your vision materialize.

Bette Nesmith Graham, divorced with a child to support, took a job as an executive secretary. An artist at heart, she fretted over messy erasures on her beautifully typed pages, so she mixed some water-based paint to match the office stationery and used an artist's brush to paint out errors. Soon every secretary wanted a supply of Bette's magic correction paint.

In 1956, she started the Mistake Out Company (later renamed Liquid Paper) and turned her kitchen into a factory. She mixed her product with an electric mixer and enlisted her son and his friends to fill the bottles. Despite working nights and weekends to fill orders, she made little money with her enterprise. Only after losing her secretarial job did she engage the time and energy that would turn her small business into a multimillion-dollar corporation. By 1968 she owned her own plant with 19 employees, and in 1979 she sold her corporation for $47.5 million.

Bette Graham didn't start out to be an inventor, but when the idea struck, she engaged, took action, managed the details of entrepreneurship and achieved stunning success. Another person may have had the same vision, but it was Bette who devoted years of engagement to develop her idea to fruition. The fun often lies in dreaming the dream, fleshing out the vision in your mind. Then come the late nights, early mornings and working weekends, getting your hands dirty with the details. That's when the casually engaged fall slack while the tenaciously persistent grab the prize and run.

Success starts with passionate vision, but engagement in a hundred thousand tiny details is the difference between success and failure.

SHRUG OFF RESTRICTIONS

While you can't simply ignore your weaknesses, you will get more value by focusing on your strengths. Improving every minor deficiency reaps little benefit.

If living your passionate vision requires a skill or knowledge you don't possess, engage it. Engagement means using all your available resources to accomplish your goals. That includes digging deep into your reservoir for outside resources to fill in the gaps. When Bette needed extra hands to fill bottles, she enrolled her son and his friends. That's being resourceful. A woman with a great idea may not be the best person to execute that idea. The global visionary may find it intolerable to focus on the details, while the perfectionist may be too detail focused to keep the big picture in mind. Look for a consultant, a subcontractor, a part-time employee or even a partner to round out your talents.

A friend of mine has all the talent to be a clothing designer, but she lacks business savvy. This is not a criticism; in the cutthroat and complicated clothing industry superb talent alone is not enough. For her, success might lie in finding the expert who can manage the mass production, promotion and distribution that will turn her fashion genius into a business success. One way or another, such details must be handled. A passionately intuitive woman will shrug off restrictions and engage the necessary resources.

BE YOUR OWN LOTTERY

At age 28, I started my business while working a full-time job. While my friends spent their nights and weekends partying, I worked nights and weekends on my fledgling enterprise, determined to succeed at my new venture. After my business was running smoothly, I went to law school. That took up nights and weekends for four more years. Staying engaged wasn't always easy, and no one held my hand or cracked the whip. I had to be my own taskmaster.

Despite my taxing schedule I always gave my clients more than they expected. In my home state of Louisiana, we call it lagniappe, a little something extra. That lagniappe came back tenfold in client loyalty, which translated into security, success and dollars. I spent hard years paying my dues, and one woman suggested I'd missed a lot of "pop culture." I don't feel I missed anything; and now I get to play a lot, enjoying my passions. I made myself a millionaire while others partied.

Too many people expect the payoff without paying in. That's why casinos and the lottery are so popular, because people want the winnings without the work.

I believe in creating my own lottery. The harder I work, the luckier I get. I ensure my success by going beyond what most people are willing to do. So did Daryn Kagan when she took a job as a sportscaster, a woman in a man's world. She committed to working weekends without pay. That's far more than anyone at the television station expected, and she hit the jackpot down the line.

DON'T BE A COMMITMENT QUEEN

When I first started my seminars, I engaged to the point of exhaustion. I taught all day, and I always had lunch with the students. At day's end, they invited me to dinner, which was not a relaxing affair because I was still the teacher and they'd want to pick my brain. Finally, my sister Karen asked me, "Vickie, why don't you say no, take some time for yourself and relax a little?" Eureka—I started setting boundaries and learned that people are usually okay with them.

Women are queens of commitment. In fact, I'm cautious when speaking to women about commitment, because women tend to overcommit. We can also be tenacious about overcommitting to the wrong people and the wrong goals. We martyr ourselves beyond reasonable engagement. No wonder we're so exhausted. What's interesting is that once I set the dinner boundary, people stopped inviting me to dinner. It was as if I had sent a subliminal message. They got it. They easily accepted it.

Engagement doesn't require giving up yourself and subordinating your dreams to help friends and family achieve theirs. We all need to set boundaries on our willingness to engage.

Engage to Achieve Big Things with the

5 PROMISES

PROMISE 1

I Will Live and Work a Passionate Life

What Big Thing must you engage now to live your passionate vision?

_____

_____

_____

What commitments must you let go?

_____

_____

_____

PROMISE 2

I Will Go for It or Reject It Outright

What fear must you overcome to accomplish this Big Thing? How will you use momentum sessions to break the feel-good addiction?

_____

_____

_____

*P*ROMISE 3

I Will Take One Action Step a Day Toward My Passionate Vision

Identify three action steps you will take to accomplish your Big Thing. Specifically, when will you tackle your momentum sessions each day? Which tasks will you designate as weeds?

_____

_____

_____

*P*ROMISE 4

I Commit to Being a Success Student for Life

What areas of training or knowledge would assist you in accomplishing your Big Thing? How and when you will gain this knowledge?

_____

_____

_____

*P*ROMISE 5

I Believe as a Woman I Really Can Do Anything

Identify a fear you overcame and the risks you took to do so. What did you learn that will help you achieve your Big Thing?

_____

_____

_____

Download the 5 Promises for Engagement at InsideEveryWoman.com.

LEIGH'S ENGAGEMENT

A bookstore owner I met early in my publishing career invited me to my first Houston Financial Council for Women luncheon meeting. The women who gathered for this networking meeting wore perfect accessories and drank wine. They all seemed so sophisticated and self-assured. I was in my 20s and not one bit sophisticated. I wanted to be like them, so I applied for membership. I wasn't a powerful networker, but I attended every meeting and that got me noticed. A huge part of success is showing up, but I didn't know that then.

A member I admired was elected president and asked me to serve on her board. Who, me? I was flattered but unsure, having never served on any board, but she guaranteed I could do it. That was the beginning of my commitment to advance professional women, and I became totally engaged.

As program director, I brought in Ann Richards, before she was elected governor of Texas, to speak to our small group. As vice president of membership, I created information packets for potential members. I discovered the reward of always giving a little extra. As president, I introduced our organization into a larger arena, the

Federation of Houston Professional Women, an alliance of women's organizations similar to ours.

Again, I showed up. I volunteered on Federation committees and proved I could be counted on. Just nine months after joining, I became a member of their impressive 20-member board. I gave hours to my cause when I didn't have money. As membership director, I spoke to women's associations all over Houston to encourage them to join. My passion to engage women resulted in 18 new member organizations—twice as many as previous directors had brought in. When I lost my first bid for president, I continued my engagement and served on the winner's board as newsletter editor, where I expanded the format, increased the number of pages and sold more ads than anyone else. Four years after joining, I was elected president of this 6,000-member organization.

I get a charge out of making interesting and valuable connections for women. If someone mentions that she needs an interior designer or banker or computer repair, I know who she can call. I am continually engaged in promoting the success of businesswomen in our community. Engagement is easy when you are passionate.

*L*EIGH,
a woman who doesn't tell her age
Marketing Director

Engagement gives you momentum to live your passionate vision, and you'll engage momentum at ever higher levels using the feminine force of agility, which we'll explore next.

> *Do something every day that scares you.*
> —Eleanor Roosevelt

If we don't change, we don't grow.
If we don't grow, we aren't really living.
—Gail Sheehy

When you stretch yourself in what you're afraid to do,
the next challenge isn't nearly as scary;
the ground is more familiar.
—Vickie L. Milazzo

$\mathscr{A}$GILITY

Flex Your Agility to Grab New Opportunities

Women's bodies are naturally more flexible than men's. Just go to any beginners' yoga class and watch the men. Then watch the women. Men have their own strengths, but women are naturally engineered for agility.

Also more mentally agile, women tend to be excellent at multitasking. Gather any group of women with a variety of talents, emotions and intelligence, and you'll find that most of them are juggling a dozen different projects. Women are flexible and adaptable.

In prehistoric times women had to use both sides of their brains. Women and men participated almost equally in hunting and gathering food. As agriculture developed, women prepared the food, made clothing and cared for children while also plowing fields, harvesting crops and tending animals. Later, as people gathered into cities, women sold or traded goods in the marketplace. So very early on we developed the agility to be well rounded in our skills and expertise.

Being agile, a woman can change directions quickly, take advantage of opportunities, try new alternatives and be perfectly okay with making mistakes. She accepts challenge and embraces conflict when necessary. A passionate, agile woman never says "I can't" when it comes to achieving her goals. She knows that success comes in "cans," that when faced with challenge, every "can't" she utters will limit her agility and her ultimate success.

Agility is the path to a deeper, richer experience. The more we stretch, the deeper we're able to go into our passionate vision. This is true not only with our bodies but with our minds and the goals we pursue. When we challenge ourselves to stretch, our physical, mental and emotional energy revs up to make anything possible. Agility enables us to recognize when we're rigidly holding onto commitments that no longer reinforce our vision. It's the ability to initiate the changes imperative to living passionately.

Imagine watching an ant carrying a piece of straw that seems too big a burden. Coming to a crack in the earth too wide to cross, the ant stands for a time as though pondering the challenge, then places the straw across the crack and walks over it.

This ant gives us two quick lessons: (1) agility is admitting that a path isn't working and changing it, and (2) agility turns a burden into a bridge for progress. The challenges that accompany change are a gift of agility lifting you to the next level. They make what once was difficult come easy. As with physical exercise, challenges expand your agility for moving through life with ease and confidence.

SHAKE IT UP

To be highly successful at anything, you must be willing and able to go new places, change directions, shake things up. Risking even minor change strengthens your agility to go where you need to go next and prepares you for major challenges later that will undoubtedly require even more change.

When I find myself resisting disruption in my life I try to remember that soon I will see this challenge as the barrier that, once crossed, opened a gate to new perspectives, new opportunities and new choices. I will look back and see how risking change presented an opportunity to become more agile.

Effective change requires fire, vision and courage. Women have proved time and again to have ample courage. Courage is simply another choice we make.

Effective change also requires discipline. It takes discipline to continually risk following your vision despite setbacks. It takes discipline to develop new habits of agility.

Every morning, while showering or getting dressed, ask yourself, "What's not working as well as it could in my life? What might work better? And how will I change it?" Then implement that positive change, no matter how small.

A speaker I know consulted a voice coach to improve her natural monotone, which threatened to put audiences to sleep. The coach taught her to exaggerate the words, to elaborately roll the *r*'s, bite down hard on the consonants and round out the vowels, to shout, whisper, sob, to be more than dramatic, to be melodramatic. After stretching to these exaggerated limits, her voice, like a rubber band, expanded and became more flexible, until a middle ground of varying emphasis and intensity came naturally. Her natural voice never returned to the stiff monotone.

When we welcome change and expand our agility, we realize that what we thought of as our "natural state" will never return to its former stiff and monotonous self. We find ourselves in a new space of unlimited options.

It's easy to believe that only a certain type of charismatic person will be massively successful. But I remember as a child being teased about my imaginary classes. My older sister, the popular girl, and my twin brother, the celebrated athlete, thought I was the nerdiest kid ever. I was quiet, reserved and serious, exactly the opposite of charismatic. I always had a mission. My girlfriends changed their baby dolls while I plotted to change the world.

As I took more and more risks, diving deeper into areas I'd never been, I lost that timidity. When you take a risk and accept the challenge of change, you stretch yourself in what you're afraid to do. You build reserves of courage that will grow with you. The next challenge isn't nearly as scary, because it isn't out there so far. The ground is more familiar, the obstacles don't loom as large and you're more agile in scaling them.

FLEX YOUR CURIOSITY

I've already confided to you my fear of heights. Now you'll think I'm a bundle of total trepidation as I reveal another fear: water. A near-drowning experience when I was a child left me wary of swimming and totally unwilling to go deeper than snorkeling along the water's surface.

Before Tom and I went to Fiji, he had already been scuba diving many times during the preceding five years. I'd heard his fun stories, but I knew he still occasionally experienced anxiety due to a long-ago diving incident. Tom, the daredevil, with all his diving experience, having anxiety? That made it even harder for me to decide to go for it. The only way I would venture out on the dive boat was with the promise to myself that I could choose not to go in the water.

Upon arrival at the reef, the first thing the dive master talked about was sharks. "This is their world. They're in control. Don't approach or move toward them. Respect them. Respect their space." Actually, sharks didn't scare me at all. I was too afraid of the water to worry about sharks. First I had to get into the water. Then I'd think about sharks.

Several years earlier, on Maui, I had tried to learn to dive. On that first attempt Tom, my 14-year-old nephew Matt and I started our lessons in the pool. As soon as the water closed over my face mask and I struggled with the weight of the tank and BCD vest that threatened to drown me, I climbed out of the pool and didn't look back. Within the safety of the shore, I enjoyed a massage instead. While the guys took to the ocean like fish, exploring coral reefs, shipwrecks and the limitless variety of sea life, I clung to my beach chair with my self-help book.

On later vacations Tom and I worked out a compromise. He would dive, then return to snorkel with me. Although not much of a swimmer, I was a great flailer. I snorkeled in the shallows, where I could stand up when I tired from flailing or needed to adjust my mask. Yoga practice had prepared me for proper breathing and body control, and over time my confidence grew. So did the quality of my flailing. To this day my nephew calls me shark bait.

Back to Fiji: I watched a young girl with a mental disability go out doggedly every day learning to dive, while I stayed safely on the surface, afraid to leave my shallow comfort zone for the deeper unknown. I wondered who had the greater disability, she or I. Hers was real, mine only imagined. Who was more agile?

Every afternoon, Tom regaled me with stories of turtles, lionfish, hammerhead sharks and the vibrant coral he saw on his dives while I continued flailing about in the shallows. But each day I snorkeled into deeper and deeper water until finally, on day four, I built up the confidence to approach the edge of a 300-foot wall. Looking into its depths I was suddenly no longer content to observe from the surface. My curiosity engaged, I longed to dive deep and envelope myself in the dark wonders below. I resolved to try diving again.

My first dive was in a shallow bay. I clung to the bottom, pulling up sand and sea grass at 15 feet down. Easy. Being close to the bottom gave me security and perspective, and the small success encouraged me to go for more.

The second day I dove longer and deeper to 25 feet. On my third day of diving, we boated to a sandy ledge that led to the 300-foot wall I was ready to explore. The boat rocked on five-foot swells. Tom and the dive master rolled off the side of the boat backwards—the standard diver's show-off entry. When the dive master instructed me to do the same, I said, "No way!" and headed down the narrow stepladder designed for deck shoes, not fins. No easy feat. Tom said it was typical of me to take the hard way down. Stepping from the ladder, I slid beneath the surface.

After the initial roller coaster ride associated with equalizing my ears and my anxiety, we swam along the shallow bottom to the precipice and slowly dropped into the 300-foot abyss. Surprisingly, the stability and quiet of being underwater was a wonderful respite from the swells that bounced the boat on the surface. Anyway, it does no good to scream underwater.

I was grateful that my beginner's depth was limited to 45 feet, but swimming along the side of the wall I was still clearly in another world, with nothing under my fins but darkness.

Soon I was keenly observing the sea life. Coral heads, bulbs, fans and thousands of fish, all sizes and temperaments, from the diminutive clown fish bravely defending his anemone home, to the shy 35-pound sweetlips, who disappeared into his coral cavern at the first sight of us. My dive master floated serenely behind me, arms crossed, conserving breath and energy. Only his fins were moving, even when the menacing 10-foot reef sharks swam past us.

As my breathing became more relaxed and quiet, I began to hear the sounds of the sea life. Midway, Tom joined me, held my hand in celebration, and I lost all sense of time, depth and my childhood fear. While I'll never be a fish in the water, I was now enjoying their world. Even more, I was enjoying my newfound agility.

CHALLENGE A FIXED VIEWPOINT

Where would I be if I hadn't challenged my fear of water? Probably where I am now, but with less confidence. I believe the happiest people are those who are always growing and stretching. The only way to grow is to question, challenge, probe for new answers and be agile enough to try new things.

In business, you grow or you die. Most of us are willing to stretch when it comes to our careers. It's expected. You strive for a bigger paycheck, a bigger office, more influence or more power. Why don't we do the same in our personal lives? One always affects the other.

In life, as in business, when you neglect growth, the passion inside you cools. Plan not only for a bigger house or an updated vehicle, but for inner growth. Try to reinvent yourself on a regular basis. You don't want to wake up five years from now and greet the same person in the mirror. You want to see a woman who has transcended her former boundaries. Refusing to grow and stretch keeps you locked in a box of your own making, just as not taking that dive might have kept me out of the deep underwater world for the rest of my life. We set up our own failure when we believe those insidious mantras, "I can't . . . I don't . . . I wasn't trained for that."

A woman in one of our seminars who was struggling with the fast-paced training became upset because she couldn't record the program. I offered to let her leave the seminar that day and take with her the DVD program to study at her own pace.

She refused the offer. Instead, she sat on the front row the entire six days talking to herself, escalating her frustration and not listening to a word of the seminar. At the end of the program, she was one of only a few people who failed the certification examination. She had sabotaged herself by self-talk. Perceiving her condition to be less than perfect, she created, then reinforced, those perceived conditions. Even if the class seemed overwhelming, she could have dramatically improved her experience by challenging her fixed viewpoint.

That's not to say we should shut our eyes to problems. Agility comes in recognizing what's not working and fixing it. But there's a difference between complaining or stirring up unrest and pointing out a situation that needs to be changed. When employees come to me with a complaint, I say, "Don't criticize—strategize and offer an alternative." I don't expect the perfect solution, but I do expect a suggestion.

I didn't always own a company. I grew up selling Avon, working at Burger King and then working in hospitals. Entrepreneurship constantly challenges my viewpoints and has taught me this attitude: "Wherever you are, make the most of it by questioning, probing and challenging fixed viewpoints." Add a sense of wonder and curiosity. The more you open up to the amazing world around you, the more agility you will have.

I could easily have enjoyed Fiji without flexing my agility beyond snorkeling, but after I challenged my viewpoint, Fiji became
an unforgettable, life-changing experience. Inside every woman
is the agility to be anything she wants to be and to do everything
her passionate vision demands.

STRETCH TO INTENSIFY AGILITY

I thought diving to 45 feet was a big deal until I learned there are
divers who go 11 times deeper without scuba gear. Imagine taking
one huge breath and plunging hundreds of feet into the ocean, so
deep you need a light to see where you're going. Just try holding
your breath for six minutes!

This dangerous sport attracts a surprising number of women.
"No-limits" free divers ride a weighted sled to the target depth
and swim back to the surface—all on a single breath. The no-
limits women's record was set by Tanya Streeter in 2002, who
dived to 525 feet and back in 3 minutes 26 seconds—deeper than
many submarines reached during World War II.

Mandy-Rae Cruickshank set the record depth of 255 feet for
women's "constant-weight" diving in 2004. The constant-weight
free diver uses only a pair of fins and propels herself alongside a
guideline to her target depth. She depends entirely on her own
strength, swimming incredibly hard while using minimal oxygen
and exertion, each movement as graceful and fluid as a dolphin's.
She wastes no energy; every bit goes into pushing toward her goal.

Strong, agile women are like Mandy-Rae and Tanya, willing
to dive deep into their dreams, visions, desires and fears. Challenge yourself. It's important to have realistic goals, like losing
five pounds or selling 15 percent more, but you should also have
a stretch goal that's out there on the horizon. Stretching intensi-

fies agility. Go for it. I'd much rather set one audacious goal and
not quite reach it than set all my goals too low. Expanding and
intensifying agility prepares you for bigger opportunities you'll
encounter as your new passionate life unfolds.

DIVE DEEPER EVERY DAY

Record-breaking free divers practice their skills until they become
automatic. Their amazing agility comes from setting aside a huge
portion of their lives for training, planning, preparation and
execution.

To survive such extremes, to break records and safely return to
the surface, a free diver pushes to new limits on deeper and deeper
training dives. For a dive lasting mere minutes, she might endure
10 months of training. She runs, lifts weights, diets, practices
holding her breath and achieves startling levels of concentration
to extend one breath even further than ever before.

My company has grown every year. I attribute this growth to
our continuously going deeper into our passionate vision and ma-
neuvering with agility. We add new layers and new depth through
training, planning, preparation and execution. We make sure that
we're working effectively—smarter, not harder. We constantly ask
ourselves if there's a better way to do what we're doing. Can we be
more flexible, more responsive to opportunity? As a result of this
constant agility training, we can dive deeper with every breath.
We never settle for ordinary when another stretch might take us
to extraordinary. While our 15 percent growth is better than average, the real gain comes in the cumulative effect. Growing even 7
percent, personally or in business revenues, might not sound like
a big deal, but do that every year for 5, 10 or 30 years and you'll
find yourself in an awesome place that's not crowded.

What are the skills that will take you to the next level in living your passionate vision? Like the free divers, you must be willing to invest time and energy in training until your skills become deeply ingrained, then maintain those skills so that you can access them with agility as needed.

For a free diver, taking the correct action instinctively, with the lightning speed that a prepared mind is capable of, can make the difference between survival and drowning. When you face a challenge in your personal life or career, your skills and knowledge will serve you well—if you've practiced until you instinctively make good choices.

To dive deep you must focus on a few things, not on everything. My company, for example, could create continuing education in hundreds of nursing specialties, but we choose not to. We train and certify registered nurses as Certified Legal Nurse Consultants. Why? First, because our students see us as the true experts we are; we don't dabble all over the place. Second, because this is our passion. This is what we do best.

In today's world we are bombarded with so many options that it's difficult to choose where to focus. The deeper you dive, the narrower your choices. Choose a few areas in which you passionately want to improve your agility and focus on diving deep.

AGILITY IS A TWO-MINUTE INVESTMENT

On an eight-hour red-eye flight from Amsterdam to Nairobi I realized I was destined to suffer severe sciatica during my African photo safari unless I quickly made a change. My backpack held what I perceived to be the solution, an inflatable seat cushion I had packed for the long jeep rides. Being five feet two inches, I asked Tom to help me retrieve the backpack from the overhead bin.

A quick note about Tom: He's the hunker-down-with-a-book-and-don't-move pulmonary-embolism type of air traveler. He takes the window seat, which is great because he never climbs over you, but it makes him resistant to any requests that involve getting up once he takes that seat, which he does immediately upon boarding.

"Are you sure you want to pull that cushion out of your pack?" His question might have sounded reasonable to a stranger, but 13 years of marriage enabled me to quickly translate: *Now that we're seated with our drinks, mixed nuts and magazines, are you sure you want me to unbuckle my seat belt, stand up and haul your pack out of the overhead, so you can remove everything in it to get to the cushion stashed at the bottom, only to have to repeat the process to repack the cushion two minutes later?*

"Yes! It's worth a try. Two minutes against the discomfort of this entire flight is an easy trade-off." Tom grudgingly agreed, and it worked. That two-minute investment paid off with eight hours of comfort plus an enjoyable, sciatica-free vacation.

Of course, it might not have worked at all. The point is, I was willing to invest my time (and Tom's energy) in attempting a solution. Agility often means experimenting today in hopes of success tomorrow. Agility comes from a willingness to try something different.

Similarly, agility means investing now for payoff tomorrow. When you know you need to initiate a change, avoid spending time thinking of reasons not to. Think about anything long enough and you'll come up with dozens of reasons against it. Focus on the payoff, then just stretch and do it.

Are you investing today in your growth for tomorrow? Or are you resisting a simple change that could pay off big down the line? Investing now for eventual success requires time and effort. Even inflating a cushion takes lung power. Invest two minutes today, five minutes tomorrow. Small investments in your growth pay big dividends when you need that agility later.

SCHEDULE AN AGILITY BREAK

Because free divers are going where nobody has gone before, they're free to make up their own training rules to break more records. They're free to break out of accepted routines and do what works best. That's true for entrepreneurs too, who are the masters of agility in business. To strengthen your agility, break some routines in your career and personal life. The value in routine is that it conserves energy. As we learn from our mistakes, we develop routines that facilitate speed and accuracy. Attacking new problems with a familiar and successful system saves time and other resources. We get into a groove. Routine can also be a source of confidence as we accept new risks.

But routine will be the enemy of your agility if you're not alert. At the gym, if I do the same workout, without adding new challenges to my muscles, they get so used to it that I stop advancing. I have to shift, do a different exercise, get off the stairclimber, get on the treadmill or take that six-mile walk in the park. We need to be agile mentally and emotionally as well as physically. Routine can quickly become a rut that we dig deeper and deeper simply to avoid risking a new path.

Be spontaneous and break your routine by doing something you wouldn't normally do. Get out of your ordinary world and experience what else is out there. Think of an activity you've always wanted to try but resisted. Perhaps you never felt you had the time, or you found it too frightening, or you feared embarrassment if you failed. This might be a one-time thrill, such as riding in a hot air balloon. It might be an artistic challenge, such as quilting or sketching. It might be ice skating or tennis.

Mark an appropriate time block in your calendar for your appointed change in routine. Let go of excuses and "I can't." Yes, even busy women can find a few minutes or an hour to increase agility. There is no right time, except now. When the moment comes, enjoy the adventure. If you're tempted to allow "more important" tasks to replace this spot on your calendar, don't.

Hang out with people who are different from you. One of my best friends from high school asked me one day, "Vickie, did you ever wonder how we got to be such great friends when we're so different?" While I excelled in business, Missy excelled in being a great mom. While I'm excessively neat, she doesn't mind a little clutter. She might say that I have better taste in men; I'd say she has a better gift of gab.

Opening your mind and energy to people who have different talents, opinions and lifestyles can introduce you to new ideas and new ways of solving problems. When choosing your support team, consider people of varying age, interests, attitude, education, background and social level. They will shake up your thinking, encourage you to step out of your routines and enhance your willingness to take new risks.

DON'T BE A RELIC OF PAST SPLENDOR

Angkor Wat is the relic of an ancient civilization that was far advanced for its time. On a trip to Cambodia I was blessed to spend three days exploring the ruins of this magnificent complex of temples, many built more than 900 years ago. These relics of past splendor were created with stones carried from far away and constructed without modern machinery. Yet the structures have withstood the ravages of time, weather and mankind.

In contrast, on my last evening in Cambodia, I took a boat ride through Chong Khneas, a floating fishing village. This loose collection of more than 700 families of fishermen and a complete support community live on boats and travel Tonlé Sap Lake following the fish and the rainy season. To reach it we drove along an unpaved road through villages with primitive living conditions. Bamboo shacks stood on spindly poles to withstand flooding. I would have been afraid to roll over in my sleep in these houses, much less raise a family or ride out a monsoon in one. Electricity was nonexistent, and the only running water was the stream we were following to the lake. The only nod to the 21st century was televisions, running on car batteries and prominently displayed in glassless windows.

The floating village consisted of hundreds of boats, some no bigger than 20 feet by 6 feet. Entire families lived on each boat. Cages suspended underneath the boat served as impromptu fish farms. The back of the boat held a primitive outhouse. Children bathed in the lake while old women cleaned fish or cooked noodles in water dipped from the same source. The lake served not only as a source of food and of cooking and drinking water, but as the bathtub and septic system as well. Here the ubiquitous televisions, and the outboard motors used to power the fishing boats onto the lake each evening, were the only lifestyle changes in the last 200 years.

The floating village and the bamboo shacks were light years below the standard of living enjoyed by the Cambodians who designed and lived in the temple complex at Angkor Wat. All of those past splendors seem lost today.

What lesson can we learn from this study in contrasts? How did these people lose touch with the agility of spirit and intelligence that made Angkor Wat possible? Instead of stretching forward, they idle in place.

Once we cease to learn, build, create and stretch, we not only stop gaining or growing, we allow the rest of the world to pass us by. Ask yourself frequently, "Am I moving forward or simply drift-ing?" The lesson I learned in Cambodia is that agility comes when you learn from the past while stretching steadily and passionately forward. Don't be a floating relic of past splendor.

LEAVE YOUR OLD COMFORTS AT HOME

When packing for a trip to the deserts of Morocco I noticed that I was cramming in an awful lot of American comforts. I tend to travel like the old British explorers: teapot, table, tent and a Sherpa or two.

Having invested a lot of time and money in the adventure of exploring this exotic destination, I had to laugh at myself. I thought, "If I'm going to bring the U.S. with me, I might as well stay at home." By replicating my homey comforts, I would actually miss what I was going in search of—an exciting, unpre-dictable experience that would enliven my senses, stimulate my creative juices and move me out of my comfort zone so that I could return home rejuvenated, with increased agility to deal with all the challenges of life and business. I didn't need my blow-dryer to ride a camel and sleep in the Sahara desert. By leaving such items behind, I packed lighter and was able to immerse myself in the Moroccan culture with a more complete sense of adventure.

Isn't this how we often approach life, dragging old baggage into new situations? We decide to travel to a new place—a new career, a new relationship. But we carry along old attitudes that deny us the new experience.

In your passionate new life, you'll be traveling to a new place, so leave your old comforts at home. The less baggage you carry, the more opportunity you'll have to flex your agility. Pack a lighter bag.

Flex Your Agility with the

5 *P*ROMISES

*P*ROMISE 1

I Will Live and Work a Passionate Life

In what way do you need to be more agile to dive deeply into your passionate vision?

_____

_____

_____

*P*ROMISE 2

I Will Go for It or Reject It Outright

What risk will you take to stretch to your new level of agility?

_____

_____

_____

*P*ROMISE 3

I Will Take One Action Step a Day Toward My Passionate Vision

Write down two action steps you will take to stretch to the next level.

_____

_____

_____

*P*ROMISE 4

I Commit to Being a Success Student for Life

Define a third level of growth, a stretch that seems unattainable.
How, when and where will you attain the knowledge or training to
reach this advanced level of agility?

_____

_____

_____

*P*ROMISE 5

I Believe as a Woman I Really Can Do Anything

Focus on your highest aspiration. See yourself enjoying the attainment
of this highest goal, then reach out with your inner being for a tangible
symbol of attainment. What is that symbol? Write it down.

_____

_____

_____

Listen with your inner ear to the praise and congratulations of your
peers, family and friends. (Reject any negatives.) What are they saying?

_____

_____

_____

Download the 5 Promises for Agility at InsideEveryWoman.com.

BLANCHE'S AGILITY

I learned so much from my mom, especially how to make do, how to be agile. We didn't have a lot of money, but my mom was a very strong and agile woman. We raised chickens and sold eggs. My mom made dresses out of feed sacks for me to wear. She loved to sew. I had all these fancy dresses, which made everyone think we were rich. One day, I asked my mother, "Are we poor?" She replied, "No, you will never be poor. You can be broke but not poor. You are rich because you have family, love and food to eat."

My husband passed away six months ago from strokes he'd had for years. Before that he was ill a lot. Every day was a challenge for him, and for me as I figured out how to help him eat, walk and communicate. I had to entertain and humor him, keep him emotionally stable.

We all have choices in life. I chose to stand by him no matter what. It wasn't easy. I worked as a dental assistant for 34 years and was the sole supporter of my family. I did what I had to do. Surrounding myself with all the kids in the neighborhood kept me young and agile. You can either make life good or not. I try to be agile and open-minded, try to see humor in everything. You've got to have lightness and darkness. How would we know what lightness feels like if we didn't have darkness to remind us?

I'm a woman, I'm strong and rich in the ways that count and I know how to do more than just get by. I choose to celebrate even when I feel like crying. That's agility. I guess I'm lucky I grew up in New Orleans, where you don't need a reason to celebrate.

*B*LANCHE, 74
A lover of life, people and trees

With agility you can tackle a world of options as you follow your passionate vision. The next feminine force, the genius inside every woman, can make your vision a brilliant reality.

Those curve balls are always coming.
Eventually, you learn how to hit some of them.
—Queen Latifah

The especial genius of women I believe to be electrical in movement, intuitive in function, spiritual in tendency.
—Margaret Fuller

Genius is not fixed but elastic.
—Vickie L. Milazzo

GENIUS

Intensify Your Intelligence for Accelerated Success

Study after study shows that, overall, men and women are equally intelligent. Interestingly, women's grade point averages in college are generally higher than men's, no matter what field they study. The proportion of women completing college has topped that of men, and the lead is widening. And after the age of 30 a higher percentage of women than men continue their education, whether or not they have previously earned a degree.

Although equally intelligent, men and women have different kinds of intelligence. Women have smaller, more compact brains with more gray matter, which tends to improve efficiency. Men have more white matter, which makes them more adept at spatial tasks and thus enhances their athletic abilities. Women typically excel at verbal tasks.

In my experience, women's intelligence tends to be broader than men's. Men are more intellectually focused. Women use their holistic intelligence to accumulate knowledge in more areas and to synthesize that material. In the "total immersion" process of learning, women take it in all at once, through our eyes, ears and intuitive senses.

What does all this mean? It means that despite historical data citing more male "geniuses," women can do anything intellectually that men can do. We simply do it differently.

WOMEN INGENIOUSLY COLLABORATE

Tom and I went on a fishing retreat in the Colorado backcountry with a group of CEOs and their spouses. I was one of only two women CEOs in the bunch. One evening we decided to play a game, the men against the women. On opposite sides of a blazing campfire, each team asked the other trivia questions from a list about the opposite gender. The men might ask, "Who's Earl Anthony?" The women, "What's GWP?"

The two teams used completely different approaches. The women huddled and collaborated on the answers as well as the questions. I whispered, "Tom's going to know that GWP means gift with purchase. Every time I buy cosmetics I show him my gift and brag, 'I got my GWP!'" The other women chimed in, and together we strategically decided which questions to ask. In contrast, the men studied their list of questions individually. When a man's turn came, he asked the question he perceived to be hardest. No collaboration, and total astonishment when the women got it right. One question was about weight lifting. As soon as a man asked it, Tom exclaimed, "Arghhh!" He knew I'd know that answer, but since the guys didn't collaborate, Tom's information was useless. The men also popped off their answers without collaboration.

A team of highly successful CEOs against mostly homemakers—wouldn't you expect the men to have the intellectual edge? To their credit, they caught on late in the game, but we still kicked their butts. And yes, we even knew that Earl Anthony was the first professional bowler to earn one million dollars during his career.

While I ultimately make my own decisions, collaboration is one of the secrets to the success of my company. Inside every woman is a natural collaborator. That's an advantage we have, a woman's intellectual edge in problem solving.

COLLABORATION IS COLLECTIVE GENIUS

The first person to receive Nobel Prizes in two different scientific fields was Marie Curie. The first, and one of the largest, pasta factories in the world was also started by a woman, Giulia Buitoni, in 1827 in Sansepulcro, Italy. Muriel Siebert takes pleasure in being the first woman stockbroker on the New York Stock Exchange. These are just a few of the sensationally intelligent and successful women ready to be your teacher if you study them.

So much to learn—so little time. Why choose the hard way when you can choose the quicker, easier path to success? Don't we always say, "I wish I'd known when I was 20 what I know now?" When we're 80, we'll be saying, "I wish I'd known when I was 40 what I know now." Find a 40-year-old and an 80-year-old and collaborate. Leverage for yourself what others have already learned. Just as you become a better tennis player by playing with tennis players who are better than you, so too will you become better at your career or any endeavor by interacting with people who are already successful in that area.

Collect gray matter wherever you can find it. There's not a single problem you will encounter that someone hasn't already successfully solved.

People often ask me, "Who's your mentor?" I can't pin it down to one person. I've been mentored by different people in different ways at different times. One person can mentor you on starting a business, another on balancing family and career. If you model or collaborate with only one person you'll always be one step behind her, but if you model many you can lead the pack.

And don't limit your collective genius to just the experts. Although experts are great, you can learn from everyone. When I bring the customer service team into the same room with marketing, finance and education, I learn more than a group of CEOs could ever teach me.

Surround yourself with as many successful mentors as you can. Choose mentors who have something interesting to say and an interesting way of saying it. Learn from their mistakes as well as their successes. Think of your mentors as a collective genius with whom you can bounce ideas around and perfect your vision. Magnify your intelligence through theirs.

Then be genius enough to actually apply what you learn. People who covet what someone else has worked hard to achieve, whether it's losing weight or making a six-figure income, often hesitate to analyze what it took to achieve those results because the answer often involves hard work and discipline.

A common question people ask me is "Vickie, where do you get the energy to manage your company and write books too?" It's true that I'm a high-energy person. I start at 4:00 a.m. and keep going until bedtime. But I don't magically wake up every morning in overdrive. There's a discipline to achieving that energy level—exercise, weight control, a good night's sleep and eating the right foods. It takes the whole routine. Yet when I tell people about that simple discipline I can see their eyes glaze over. They expect a magic potion, a quick fix like pulling out your lipstick for a touch-up.

Leveraging other people's talents is also collaborative genius. I've worked with women who say, "I want to do this all on my own." And I think, "That's crazy. Ride the horse of anybody who has what you need." I don't mean that we should take advantage of a person, but none of us arrived where we are completely on our own. That's impossible. Think about all the talented people it takes to make a movie or to care for a sick patient. Some women believe that no one can do a job the way they can. That's true. Someone might do it better.

Even when I worked solo, I leveraged other people's knowledge and talents to accelerate my future success. Whether you own a business, manage others or just manage your own day, leveraging the talents of others is just plain smart.

GENIUS HEARS OTHER VOICES

We call one extraordinary woman in our company the "other voice." When the rest of us are hot on an idea, she presents alternative ways of thinking. Without being negative, she challenges our paradigms. Recently, I sat down with my director of education and other key people to discuss a conference curriculum, expecting the discussion to go quickly. We had forgotten our other voice. She didn't like one of the choices we made. Her dissenting opinion encouraged us to revisit our decision, make significant changes and arrive at an even better result.

When we shortchange collaboration, we're missing an important piece of the performance process. As you discuss diverse opinions, ideas spark new thoughts, and one plus one suddenly equals a lot more than two. You arrive at a place neither of you would have reached alone, and your project rises to a new level.

Seek out individuals with opposing viewpoints. If you always drive a Ford, listen to the argument for driving a Nissan. If you hate opera, ask a friend who loves opera to share her insight. If you have never explored a cave and never wanted to, find a spelunker willing to give you a bat's-eye viewpoint.

There's a big difference, though, between other voices and naysayers. Naysayers can interfere with progress. I discovered this when I belonged to the CEO group. With any new concept, the reaction from the group was "No, you can't do that because. . . ." A litany of reasons followed. It's always easier to shoot holes in an idea than to conceive a workable new idea.

To gain value from the group, I had to process their feedback. In life you get a lot of feedback, but at the end of the day, sort out for yourself which advice is useful and which to ignore. While collaborating with other voices, you must ultimately heed your own.

REMOVE YOUR OWN BURRS

During a trip to Africa I went hiking with Colin Francombe on his Kenyan game sanctuary, Ol Malo. The trail varied between rock and brush. Colin's dog Shaba came with us, sometimes running ahead, other times following behind. Well into the hike we encountered a section of trail infested with burrs. Soon Shaba limped up next to me on three legs. I stooped to help.

When I asked Colin the best way to remove a burr, he replied, "Oh, I don't do that. I let her sort it out. Otherwise I'd spend all my time picking burrs off her."

I put her paw down and, sure enough, moments later she ran alongside us again on all fours, the burr gone and forgotten.

As we hiked, I considered Colin's attitude. He lives in a brutal country where self-reliance is a necessity. African people and animals learn to be strong and independent. Otherwise they'd never survive in the hostile African bush. My sympathy for Shaba's pain tempted me to intervene, and by helping her I would have made a friend for life. Instead, Colin encouraged her independence, ensuring that she'll never limp for long.

This bush survival principle also applies in our world. When we find our own solutions, we grow stronger. Excessive reliance on others weakens us. Soon we shy away from challenges we once might have conquered with relish and ease.

Consulting mentors, leveraging others' talents and listening to other voices won't protect you from every burr or help you every time you get one. Intelligent women know when to ask for help in removing burrs too big or thorny to manage alone and when to enjoy the sweet victory that comes from their own efforts. Toughen your intelligence by removing your own burrs.

GENIUS IS TRUSTING YOUR OWN VOICE

We all have an inner teacher ready to show us the way as long as we're willing to be a student of our own intelligence. In yoga class the teacher is essential, but my reflection in the mirror is my best teacher of all.

Are you a reflection of your own ideas or someone else's? Doing what others tell us to do is often a way to avoid accountability. Even though I highly appreciate brainstorm sessions and use them extensively in my company, I don't always go with the crowd. My staff teases that we're not a democracy, we're a semibenevolent dictatorship. I laugh, but I'm fine with that. The crowd is not always right. Neither am I, but at the end of the day, the decision and responsibility are mine, and they have to feel right.

Always trusting the groupthink is herd mentality. Agreeing with the majority doesn't make you right; it just means you hang out with a lot of people of like mind. They're so busy agreeing with one another that they often miss the errors in their thinking. Learn to assess your situation, evaluate for yourself and be willing to be different. Blending into the herd is not a strategy for success.

Years after I pioneered legal nurse consulting, a number of former students and other nurse consultants formed an association. I immediately started getting negative messages from them: "Vickie, you're saturating our market." "Vickie, you can't do seminars in our city." "Vickie, you can't do this, you shouldn't do that." My reaction was "I'll do it my way, thank you very much."

Nevertheless, I supported the group and tried to be part of it from a distance. Even though I knew it wasn't the right energy for me, I often recommended it to my students. When I offered to help develop a set of standards, they said, "We don't need standards." Later, I noticed they had adopted some of my standards as their own.

When our industry matured, I offered to help the association create a certification program. They again said, "No, we don't need that. We're not ready for that."

I didn't agree. While initially larger in numbers, this group didn't have my years or depth of experience. And after what had happened when I offered to help them develop standards, I knew that sooner or later they would take my idea, probably use my curriculum, and develop the certification program without me, since I wasn't a member of their herd.

I decided to create the certification program I knew our nursing specialty needed. True to form, the association developed their own several years later. In 2005 more than 1,200 nurses attended the annual conference based on my system. The herd that turned me down also held a conference, but only 450 registered. Our association has grown and prospered, while they've shrunk in membership. Their limited mindsets drive away prospective members. We advocate entrepreneurs and free thinkers while they foster an atmosphere of groupthink rigidity.

Wanting too much to be accepted as a group member or striving to please others can detract from thinking for yourself. Trust your own voice. You can enjoy the fabulous genius of collaborative thinking and still seek your own counsel.

GENIUS MULTIPLIES ITSELF

In *Yankee from Olympus,* Catherine Drinker Bowen tells the story of a woman determined to improve her mind. "Grandmother Hewett . . . at eighty-five, pink and pretty, with gentle manners and a spicy way of talking . . . taught herself to read Latin back in the times when you might wake any black night to find a tomahawk quivering in your cabin door. 'When I was a girl . . . I begged to go to school with the boys. But the elders were angry, and said Latin was not for women's heads. Go home, Tempy, they said, and learn to spin and weave. . . . So I taught myself to read Virgil. . . .'"

Tempy Hewett's commitment to fighting back in the name of intelligence at a time when education for women was downright discouraged is enviable. Learning is a lifelong engagement—a road, not a destination. To excel in today's fast-paced world, we must continuously strive for knowledge. In fact, it's predicted that the wealthy of this and future decades will be the owners of knowledge and information.

Glenda Cloud once said, "Change is inevitable, growth is intentional." You have to work at being smarter, just as you work to master a sport. To advance in a yoga posture I must be willing to lose my balance many times before my body carries me more deeply into the posture. When you aim high at learning, be prepared to be off balance, but know that you will eventually regain your balance and meet an even higher intelligence goal.

Genius is not fixed but elastic. We lose what we don't use. Frankly, most people won't exert the extra effort to get smarter. Aim high and you will seem extraordinary without a tremendous amount of effort.

A Chinese fable tells of an old man who had to cross a hill every day. Each morning at the top of the hill he took a stone in each hand and moved them to the bottom. Asked why, he said, "I'm moving this hill. Not in my lifetime or in my son's, but in time, this hill will be gone."

Like moving a hill one stone at a time, intelligence is cumulative. Think one entirely new thought and you build a new neural connection, a synapse. A multitude of synapses is what genius is made of. You may feel as though you won't accomplish in your lifetime the total expansion of mind and knowledge you want to achieve, but you're moving up the hill of intelligence. Every new synapse expands your neural network.

My dad is a young 81 because he continues to seek answers. I bought him the book *Seabiscuit* by Laura Hillenbrand, knowing he loves horse racing almost as much as he loves the casino. (I think I come in a distant third.) One day I asked if he'd finished the book. He said, "I don't have time. I've got so many other things I'm studying." Anything Dad's interested in becomes a learning obsession—whether it's Texas Hold 'em poker or the role of his new chiropractor.

Intelligent women know what they don't know and strive to learn every day. While experts suggest we should study two hours a day to keep up with new trends and technologies, even half an hour will make a measurable difference. Study any topic 30 minutes daily and watch how soon you'll become an expert. Divide study sessions into 10-minute segments with one-minute stretch breaks. We remember best what we learn at the beginning and end of a study session better than what we learn in the middle, so short segments provide more opportunities for natural recall.

Open a book. Watch a documentary. Start a study group with other lifetime success students. Smart women appreciate that what works today won't necessarily work tomorrow, and aggressive learning is a competitive advantage to achieving any desired goal. At times, your topic might be exciting and fun to learn. Other times, it's dry and arduous. In your lifelong engagement, keep in mind the Chinese fable about moving the hill and the power of small changes. Every busy schedule has at least one daily 10-minute opportunity to feed the genius within.

GENIUS COMBINES IQ AND HARD WORK

Intelligence won't get you out of doing the hard work. I learned a humbling lesson from my thesis advisor when she gave me a B in a course even though I had turned in A work. When I questioned her, she said that while the result of my semester's work was certainly A quality, I was capable of doing more than I had done. And she was right. I tried to skate through that last semester solely on my intelligence, thinking she wouldn't notice.

I was upset that she busted my 4.0 average for my master's degree, but looking back I know she did me a favor. This intelligent woman taught me that being smart is not enough. To excel in life, we have to merge IQ with a strong work ethic, which is a powerful feminine strength. Unlike our male counterparts, who often overrate their abilities, we tend to underrate ours. So we work harder. Instead we should work smarter, like Dolly Parton.

Most noted for her blonde wigs, big breasts and unique voice, Dolly is also a songwriter, entrepreneur and philanthropist. More women should heed her philosophy: "I'm not going to limit myself just because people won't accept the fact that I can do something else."

Don't be intimidated by exceptionally smart people. Conversely, don't expect a Mensa-range IQ to guarantee success. There are unemployed genius-level people out there. Thomas Edison, who failed thousands of times at producing a working light bulb before he hit on the perfect model, said: "Genius is 1 percent inspiration and 99 percent perspiration." Supplement your intelligence with hard work.

EMPLOY THE GENIUS OF EINSTEIN

Albert Einstein once said, "You can't solve a problem with the same mind that created it."

To solve a problem you've helped to create, you need to start with a new and fresh mind. For example, a woman thinks, "If I can change my job my life will be better." Possibly. But life usually doesn't work that way. That woman is likely doing and thinking the same thoughts as always. Nothing new or fresh ever gets in. If you want to effect a change, get outside yourself and look at the situation with fresh eyes. See how you might assess your problem using a different mindset.

I'm the most computer-illiterate person in my office and have no preconceived notions about what software can and cannot do. I think with an entirely different mind than our techs. Many times I ask them to make the software perform a certain way. After they tell me all their preconceived reasons why it can't, I tell them to do it anyway. Two days later the software is usually working exactly as I envisioned.

Education is wonderful, but so is forging new ground. Even though I have a string of degrees, I don't have any formal business training, which often works in my favor. I don't feel the constraints that a classroom full of MBAs all trained to think alike might feel. Not having their training, I'm free to go in any direction I choose, right or wrong.

Here are six ways to think with a different mind and improve your own in the process.

1. **Break patterns.** Insanity can be described as doing the same thing over and over and expecting a different result. Your mind is made up of neural pathways that are like roads connecting bits of information. Most of us have found ourselves walking or driving home only to jolt alert and wonder how we got there. The road is so familiar we follow it automatically. The same thing happens in your mind. Once you learn a thing and do it over and over, you follow that pathway from one thought to another automatically, which allows you to give a speech or swing a golf club.

   The mind likes patterns, and patterns are rarely easy to break. But breaking a pattern is a wonderful way to find a new solution to a recurring problem. Grocers entice us to overspend by stocking their stores in a pattern designed by shrewd marketing executives. But smart women impose their own shopping pattern, buying nonperishables first so their frozen foods don't melt on the way home. Break old thought patterns by trying new ways of doing a familiar task. Merely going to an unfamiliar coffee shop to brainstorm ideas can give you a new mindset. You'll discover fresh ways to implement new and useful solutions.

At my company's brainstorming sessions all the employees participate. We constantly change the composition of the small breakout groups. By changing the patterns, we ensure that we get different approaches every time because it's never the same minds working together.

2. *Seek new patterns.* The concept for today's computers originated with hole-punch patterns used to weave ornate jacquard fabrics. On the huge early looms, holes punched in a paper pattern allowed hooks to penetrate and grab the thread at assigned positions, creating the intricate weave. Early census takers tweaked this pattern to create hole-punched cards to record details about immigrants entering the United States. Later, IBM expanded this pattern to extraordinary levels.

Likewise, I use my nurse's diagnosing pattern (assessment, diagnosis, intervention, evaluation) to tackle issues in my business. Incorporate techniques and patterns from one discipline to creatively solve problems in another.

3. *Change a small action or behavior.* Often taking action, even a small one, will automatically change your thoughts. Instead of going immediately to your computer, if that's your habit, stop instead to write out a short list of what you want to accomplish. Then power up. You might awaken your mind to sensational new possibilities.

4. *Challenge your obstacles.* Let go of the notion that you don't have enough time, energy, money or discipline to do what it takes to succeed. Ask yourself frequently, "What beliefs, ideas and activities are obstructing my progress? What must I change to abolish these obstacles?" My biggest obstacle is believing I don't have enough time. When I challenge that thought I magically make more things happen.

5. ***Become your own other voice.*** Law school taught me to think of both sides of a problem, like boxers who anticipate their opponent's every punch. The more you anticipate opposing ideas and their impact, the better you can strategize for success and avoid fatal blows. Successful attorneys spend as much time in the mind of their opponent as they do in their own. Whether it's a career issue or a personal problem to solve, practice being your own other voice.

6. ***Influence mindset with simplicity.*** To get what we want or to achieve a goal, we frequently have to get buy-in from another person. That requires communication. An attorney taught me that there is no value in trying to win a case by proving 10 points if you can prevail by proving only 3. A case I reviewed for him involved the failure to appropriately treat a pediatric patient suffering from a traumatic head injury, which resulted in neurological damage. After I described all the parameters the ER nurse should have assessed, the attorney said, "I won't emphasize the failure to take the child's temperature. The jurors might not get the significance of that deviation." While I was technically correct in addressing this clinically important point, the lawyer was also right: He would not have to prove that deviation to win his case. Such an argument could actually backfire because a jury may be distracted from more important issues or may think he was nitpicking.

The danger in presenting too many variables for your most important communications is that your listener might lose focus and miss the entire message. Avoid making minor points that render an explanation too complex and confusing. Identify the strong points and keep coming back to those.

I learned another communication lesson from a well-known Texas plaintiff malpractice attorney who was trying a case. The young guns from the opposing team announced to their colleagues that they were "unimpressed" with the attorney's trial tactics. Yet the plaintiff attorney won a verdict of $12 million for the client. What failed to impress the less experienced counsel obviously impressed the jury. This attorney succeeded by condensing the case down to the basics, finding a focus, never straying from it and making the difficult appear simple. Twelve million dollars' worth of simple, "unimpressive" communication.

Intelligent women learn to present their ideas in such simple terms and with such vivid imagery that they create a new mindset inside the listener. Avoid distracting your listener with complexities. Break complex situations down to the most basic level and deliver a focused message.

Have you ever folded a paper airplane or an origami swan? Once someone shows the way, anyone can do it. But a discussion of the theory of airlift or the complexity of the folds without a demonstration, or at least a diagram, would likely confuse rather than clarify.

The more we focus and simplify, the more our listeners will comprehend, and the more often the desired mindset will be achieved. The process of clear communication starts and ends with us. Genius is simplicity.

Beginning today, think about which mind you have working before you tackle a challenge. Your problems won't disappear, and you may not find a solution instantly, but by keeping the possibilities in play, you allow your brain to easily hit upon a solution later. I've had to slip out of my yoga class to jot down ideas because I've had "Eureka!" moments in the middle of a pose. New patterns, new thinking, new behaviors and new communication will awaken the genius within you.

Intensify Your Genius with the

5 PROMISES

PROMISE 1

I Will Live and Work a Passionate Life

List three intelligent minds you will engage in collaboration to help you pursue your passionate vision.

_____

_____

PROMISE 2

I Will Go for It or Reject It Outright

What new mindset would enable you to passionately go all out in living your vision? What thought or belief is holding you back?

_____

_____

PROMISE 3

I Will Take One Action Step a Day Toward My Passionate Vision

From your passionate vision, select a complex idea you want to communicate. Describe it.

_____

_____

Now describe it from a different viewpoint.

_____

_____

_____

$\mathcal{P}$ROMISE 4

I Commit to Being a Success Student for Life

Invest in a book on a topic you want to know more about. Read 30 minutes a day from that book. What is your first topic?

_____

_____

_____

Subscribe to a publication outside of your industry. Read it before the next issue arrives, and apply one thing you learned to your career. Which publication will you choose?

_____

_____

_____

$\mathcal{P}$ROMISE 5

I Believe as a Woman I Really Can Do Anything

What is your spark of genius that will carry you to your passionate vision? Write down three ways to expand that genius.

_____

_____

_____

Download the 5 Promises for Genius at InsideEveryWoman.com.

CHRIS'S GENIUS

My grandmother never knew the valuable gift she gave me. Sewing or quilting, she always had a needle in hand and fabric scraps around her feet. I used a scrap to sew my doll a pair of pedal pushers—today they're called cropped pants. Even at age 10 I knew enough to cut both a front and back and to leave a seam allowance, but the pants wouldn't go on. They could easily fit a paper doll, but not a doll of any dimension. My grandmother showed me how to cut a proper pattern, which required four pieces, not two, and in that few moments I formed the first piece of a basic understanding that would direct all my future education. I realized that everything in life consisted of patterns. All I had to do was find the right pattern and I could do anything from baking a cake to one day tearing down the engine in my Datsun and replacing the head gasket.

A good student, I brought home all As except in gym, but before completing the eighth grade I dropped out to marry. By the time most girls my age were trying on high school graduation gowns, I was giving my attention to three toddlers. While I never missed the social aspects of school, I did miss the learning process, and in those early years of motherhood I hit upon the second piece of my education theory. I realized that teachers taught from books, ergo I could learn anything I wanted to learn by reading the right books. Which I did.

Along with cooking and sewing, I taught myself the concepts of design and literature. I passed the GED high school equivalency test; then, in my early 30s, I enrolled in college to get that degree I coveted. After two semesters, I looked at what I'd learned and knew that college was much too slow. I could have read dozens of excellent texts in those nine months and learned far more than I was taking away.

I never returned to college until I became a teacher, but I expanded my theory of learning to include asking questions and listening. I have been a graphic designer, illustrator and marketing consultant. I've owned a business and mentored other business owners. I've published three novels, coauthored nonfiction books and taught an adjunct mystery-writing class. I've built basic furniture and fences and painted murals. I've created and conducted seminars in writing, graphic design, photo composition and small business advertising. Every aspect of my education and the process I use to educate others has involved patterns. Thanks, Grandma.

Chris, 60
Writer and Educator

The genius inside every woman accelerates success, but only integrity will keep you at the top. Let's explore the feminine force of integrity in the next chapter.

The thinking of a genius does not proceed logically.
It leaps with great ellipses.
It pulls knowledge from God knows where.
—Dorothy Thompson

Character builds slowly, but it can be
torn down with incredible swiftness.
—Faith Baldwin

Integrity is fragile. If you compromise,
even in a small way, you become broken.
—Vickie L. Milazzo

$\mathscr{I}$NTEGRITY

Practice Uncompromising Integrity for Authentic Success

The most trusted profession is dominated by women. According to a New Jersey polling group that profession is nursing, which is 94 percent women. One of the least trusted professions, used car sales, is only 2 percent women.

Conversely, women make up less than 6.9 percent of the prison population, which tells us that on the whole women can be trusted to abide by laws and do the right thing. I cannot believe these three sets of powerful facts are accidental.

A Chinese proverb says, "If you stand straight do not fear a crooked shadow." Perhaps women stand straighter than men because we're more emotionally analytical. The emotional "why" tugs at us, and, based on our interpretation of cause and effect, we form opinions about how to act. Our interpretations feed our integrity.

A decision that seems absolutely brilliant on an intellectual level can be morally deplorable, and I believe women are more sensitive to this than men. Women inventors tend to turn out useful items such as the bulletproof Kevlar vest, fireproof housing material and machinery for factories and farms. Men also invent useful items but are equally likely to turn out inventions of destruction such as gunpowder, the guillotine or the atom bomb—or new ways to watch more sports.

As you pursue your passionate vision and reach higher, more complex levels of accomplishment—especially in your career, but also in your family development or spiritual journey—your integrity will be continuously tested in new and different ways. Think about what you would do in these situations:

✦ Coworkers at your new job get together at lunch and complain about the boss. The conversation makes you uncomfortable, but you want to be part of the group.

✦ You discover that your best friend is cheating on her husband, a man who trusts and honors her in every way.

✦ Your daughter's piano teacher singles her out for solo performances. You're delighted. Then you notice at rehearsal that another child, nearsighted and overweight, is far more talented than your adorable daughter.

Integrity-based decisions are not always easy. I've stood in the gas chamber of Auschwitz and the women's barracks at Birkenau. Visiting these horrific places, I was struck by how easily our hold on humanity can be stripped away—possessions, success, dignity, privacy and even individuality—until the only thing remaining is our personal integrity. Each day in the midst of unspeakable cruelty, the Holocaust victims had to decide how to treat others and handle themselves with integrity. Without integrity, even living through those conditions would not guarantee surviving the memories afterward. I couldn't help wondering how my own integrity would hold out in that situation.

Our choices determine whether we live a free life or a life imprisoned, and I'm not talking about a physical jail cell. No one would voluntarily imprison herself and be her own warden, yet every time we breach integrity we sentence ourselves to a mental jail.

Integrity has the final say in whether we will rise or decline, be whole or broken. When uncompromising integrity is our guide, success is authentic. And the joy of success is authentic.

BREACHING INTEGRITY
BETRAYS OPPORTUNITY

One of our seminar instructors, who was an independent contractor, was selling her products to our students while being paid to interact on our behalf. This not only violated our contract, it also violated all personal trust.

She didn't see it that way. In her mind, she was making the most of a business opportunity. When faced with a choice, to pursue quick personal sales to this ready market that we had made highly accessible to her or to honor her commitment and represent herself fully as our instructor, she elected personal gain. She was baffled when I put a halt to what she'd been getting by with. She didn't see her actions as a break with integrity.

I had to sever our business relationship entirely. Her weak character betrayed an opportunity.

Temptations abound in the business world, as they do in our personal environment. No matter how complex a decision appears on the surface, when stripped down to basics it's usually pig-simple: Do what's right, not what's most appealing.

I've had the opportunity of working with thousands of women. Many succeed and some don't, and while success is influenced by a myriad of variables, one fact stands clear: Women who persistently breach integrity don't just betray opportunities, they are broken and destined for eventual decline.

EVERY ACT COUNTS

To quote a favorite Buddhist proverb, "Even the smallest act should not be underestimated, for even tiny flakes of snow falling one atop another can blanket the tallest mountain in pure whiteness." Integrity is fragile. If compromised even in a small way, integrity is swiftly broken. Once you break integrity, it's like an avalanche—it won't stop. Cutting a corner here leads to cutting another corner there . . . and there and there. We don't burgle houses or rob banks, but do we roll through stop signs, cheat on our taxes and pocket office supplies from work?

Little things, such as not giving your all on a work project, may seem insignificant, but over time these small flakes gradually smother your passion and obscure your vision. The opportunity to demonstrate integrity can never be recaptured. A relationship that took decades to nurture can be destroyed with one frivolous breach. A career opportunity can dissolve in an instant.

Integrity compels 100 percent congruence. You can't say "I'll have integrity tomorrow but not today," or "I'll have integrity in other situations, but not in this one." Integrity is a way of living in which your mind, body and spirit unite consistently. When any part of your life is out of congruence with other parts you feel incomplete and out of sorts. Integrity is the strength that makes you whole.

Let's say you passionately accept a promotion that requires you to work excessive overtime and give up your vacation. You're also passionately committed to a family who needs you and to friends you enjoy socially. Your 70-hour workweek eats into your social time, causing you to break commitments, then it chomps away at family time, causing you to break the unspoken promise of being available and involved in your family's well-being. If you somehow manage to hold it all together, chances are you're cutting back on personal health commitments. By accepting the commitment to your career, you've broken integrity with other important parts of your life.

Congruence also applies to what you accept from others. One of my employees overheard a new hire, while filling out her initial paperwork, mumbling, "What is the name of this stupid company anyway?" The employee brought this to my attention because this remark was not congruent with our company's core values. I terminated the woman immediately. To do less would breach my company's and my own integrity.

Maintaining unwavering integrity can be tricky. Enticements and fears do sneak up on us. But at the end of the day, no matter what we've lost or gained, we need to know that our integrity is intact. We may lose our health or our money, we may outlive all our friends and family, but if we live true, we'll have the comfort that we left behind a snowy white legacy of integrity.

CONSENSUS ON INTEGRITY IS ELUSIVE

In the Female Fusion event that preceded this book, strong opinions emerged about the meaning of integrity. That discussion reinforced my belief that integrity is not easily defined and goes beyond just being honest. I found some of the comments fascinating.

Jan: It bothers me to tell even a "white lie." I was trying to explain to my nephew that you don't tell someone who has cooked dessert for you that your aunt makes a better dessert. You also don't tell her this is the best dessert you've ever had.

Vickie: Sometimes integrity means not blurting out the truth but finding a truth that's respectful and more positive. Being overly solicitous isn't the answer either; it can backfire. The mother of one of my friends is a terrible cook. This is not my New Orleans palate talking, she's just bad. Unfortunately, we often eat at her house because she likes to host family events. Everyone tells her how good her meals are—through gritted teeth. Not wanting to hurt her feelings guarantees more bad spaghetti dinners, and I never believed there could be such a thing as bad spaghetti.

Jan: Integrity is learned by example. My dad is one of the few people I know who's full of it—of integrity, that is. He set an example by always telling us the truth. If you're around people who lie and scheme, you pick up on that. Kids nowadays are picking up so much negative behavior via television.

Susan: A friend in advertising sent me an inspirational piece which read, "Integrity is saying what needs to be said, not simply what people want to hear." I really had to think about that. I'm naturally a huge people pleaser, but as an interior designer, sometimes I to have to say in a gentle way, "That looks like crap."

Chris: Following through with integrity doesn't always feel good, because you often make people unhappy.

Susan: It's going out on a limb.

Vickie: It needs to be tempered with compassion. Rose Franzblau said, "Honesty without compassion and understanding is not honesty, but subtle hostility." I find it helpful to assess my intention. We've all been the victim of the honest but mean verbal jab—it never feels good.

Chris: Expecting integrity from others, especially the people we love, is equally important. I loaned money to one of my grandsons to repair his car. He didn't finish the car and he also didn't repay the loan. I brushed it off, but I wouldn't lend him money again.

 Then his twin brother called and asked for money to retain a lawyer for a DUI. I told him I'd need to think about it, and later I said, "I'll send you the check." When he started to say, "I'll pay you back," I stopped him. "Here's what we can do: If you ever get behind the wheel of a car again after having a drink, pay me the money immediately. If you never have another drink and then drive, you owe me nothing." My intention was to avoid what happened with his brother and to also engage his integrity, which is not easy with young people.

Vickie: This sounds minor, but parents set a bad example when they slip their old popcorn bag into the movie theater to get a free refill for the bag they paid for at the last movie. Integrity is not part time. You can be semigood at playing tennis, but integrity is all or nothing.

Leigh: You don't realize how much integrity means to you until you lose it. I worked for a company built by a man who had incredible integrity. His integrity pervaded the whole com-pany. Then a different director without integrity came on board. The company is pitiful now, down to a few people. It was sad to see that company fade. When I interviewed for a new job, I knew I was not going to work for another company without integrity.

Martha: Integrity requires discipline. My grandson Cody is 12 and lives in Colorado. The last time I visited I mentioned paying the airline $75 for an oversize bag. Cody said, "Omah, you have another $75? I want to fit into your suitcase when you go back."

Cody is home-schooled, and I decided to work with him that day. He has terrible handwriting, which I'm picky about, and I made him write things over. When he read to me, he would say "a" instead of "the" or make other mistakes, and I'd tell him to read it again. It took a lot of discipline to maintain my integrity and listen to the same story three times. When we were finished Cody said, "Omah, you can spend that $75 on something else."

Leigh (laughs): He'd had enough of your integrity and discipline, and was not going home in your bag.

Martha: In the '60s, you didn't say you were a massage therapist because of the sexual connotation—and with one therapist I knew, the reputation was accurate. When he lost his license for a year, I asked him, "Why did you do it?" He said, "For the extra hundred bucks. I was behind in my rent." Later, when his business resumed, the very people who turned him in came back to him. He called me and said, "These women want the same thing again." Who had integrity there? Neither party had integrity. People have a way of stretching and justifying.

Susan: What about having integrity with ourselves? Sometimes I sell myself out, like when I promise myself Saturdays off and then take a Saturday appointment. If I break one of my personal goals I'm breaking integrity with myself.

Evie: Someone else might perceive you as not being as driven as the next person. Integrity is different for everybody. What I do might not be perceived as the right thing by someone else. Certainly there's right and wrong, but every coin has two sides. One person might seem to have integrity, then when you hear the other side, that person also has integrity. That's where I struggle with it.

Maggie: For me, it's not just about right or wrong or truth or fault. It's about living according to your standards. What is right for you might not be right for me. What you believe is good might not seem so good to me. It can be very abstract.

Vickie: In medicine, the highest principle is "first do no harm." I think that's the basis of integrity. However, each person's idea of what is harmful may differ. That's why society creates laws that set behavioral standards no matter how right a person feels about their actions.

Chris: It's interesting the way we demand upholding the law, yet believe that if a certain law is not right, it's okay to break it. We tend to cheer the lovable rascal, the charming cat burglar who steals only from the rich. He's part of our fictional culture. But we expect even a criminal to have some measure of integrity. If he ratted out his buddy or kicked a dog, we wouldn't like him any more.

Vickie: Maybe we cheer the lovable rascal because we know deep down that no matter how good our intentions, we're not perfect.

Maggie: Here in the U.S. an old lady was put in jail because she shot a burglar in the back. He was not facing her, so she had to do her time. In Honduras, an old lady shoots a burglar and she is a hero. The bad guy always has to go down. So what is integrity? You are saving your life in both examples, but in two different worlds.

Evie: Integrity is usually set by your social, cultural and religious environment. One example of my confusion with it all is something that happened to my stepfather from Mexico. When he was a young boy, his mother dishonored his father by cheating on him. It was published in the newspaper, and she was outcast by the whole community. If she had been a male, it would be just another occurrence. But they ran her out of town, and the grandmother, the husband's mother, forbid the children to ever see their mother again. I'm sure the grandmother thought she had high integrity, but to this day the children are so filled with hate for their mother that they won't get to know her. That's a conflict of integrity. It's not easy to know if you really did the right thing or if you just did the right thing for you.

Vickie: Integrity is public, not just private. I think of Hillary Clinton, who had so much power to speak to women and be a role model for strength. She copped out when she stayed married to Bill after the marriage was flagrantly violated. Women are often counseled to leave a husband who repeatedly betrays the marriage—but not, apparently, if the husband is rich, successful or president.

Hillary compounded Bill's integrity breach by overlooking it, but I still believe women are the best to protect that component. We shouldn't leave it to men to protect integrity. It is most definitely a Feminine Force.

Martha: If it had been Hillary cheating, it wouldn't have turned out that way.

Leigh: I went to a breakfast meeting where I was appalled at the foul language these smart professionals were using. It was dreadful. Afterward, when everyone at the table commented on the meeting, I told them what I thought, and that I was glad they didn't have a guest speaker that morning to be subjected to such language. I never went back.

Martha: There might have been others who felt like you but didn't honor their integrity and speak up.

Susan: Say what needs to be said, not just what people want to hear.

Martha: I was born in Switzerland, the oldest of eight children, and I was the caretaker. I did not have much opportunity to play. My siblings were like my dolls. I was proud to help my mother, but I was also determined to get what I wanted, and sometimes a little rebellious. Having responsibility for these siblings, if they did something wrong, it was my fault. This left marks that stayed with me.

Now I am a very strict instructor. I want the students to get it right. The massage method I teach is difficult to learn, takes a lot of dedication and must be performed precisely for optimal results. My students do not always like me during class, since I correct their hands so often, but they survive my class and like me afterwards. I tell them, "It's either right or wrong. I simply call it the way it is."

EVERY PROMISE COUNTS

With the best intentions, we extend ourselves in one area, perhaps our career, which causes us to unintentionally slight another: Our family, our financial well-being or our physical well-being. If you promise yourself you will absolutely take that vacation this year, but fail to follow through because you overcommitted in another area, you've betrayed your promise and yourself.

Some people might even see you as a hero for putting others' interests ahead of your own. But that failure is like the first domino in a line—one falls against the next, which falls against the next, and so on until none is left standing.

Parents learn early on that every promise to a child counts and not to overpromise. When a child asks, "Mom, can we go to the beach this weekend?" an astute mom avoids promising and will probably say, "We'll see." Otherwise, if the weekend comes and conditions aren't right, the child will still expect delivery on the promise.

The need to avoid overpromising in all relationships is a lesson I learned at high cost. When my sister and her husband came into my business, I made a promise I later could not keep. They relocated from San Diego to Houston to join Tom and me. We were working out of our house to keep the overhead low. I set up a reward incentive: as the company grew, we'd all get paid significantly more. I wanted these people, who were important to me, to benefit from our success. But that wonderful incentive was based on keeping the business in my home forever, with only the four of us as employees. It worked great at first. Within months the company grew beyond what any of us expected. We moved into an expensive office space, adding salaries and lots of other overhead. My shortsighted promise became impossible to keep.

That was a rough time for me. I didn't want to break my integrity, but I had promised a future I couldn't deliver or feel good about. I modified the bonus structure and offered my sister and her husband a full year's severance package. They accepted the severance and moved back to San Diego, which was where they really wanted to be.

A promise is usually made based on certain conditions, and conditions change. That painful life experience and the hurt we all suffered taught me to promise within boundaries.

PUT YOUR INTEGRITY WHERE YOUR MOUTH IS

Any time anyone makes a negative comment about a person not present, that's gossip. Gossip is not just mean; it's a break with integrity that hurts us as much as the object of the gossip. Gossip also wastes time and energy.

Like most people, I'm challenged by the commitment to never gossip, so Tom and I created a way to not get sucked into it. When confronted with gossip, one of us will say, "Well, you know Mary's not here to defend herself." That remark will usually stop the gossip cold, without putting anyone on the spot. I say it in a fun, friendly manner, with a smile, but it clearly lets the gossiper know I don't intend to go there, and if she goes there, she'll have to do it without me.

Perhaps you have the integrity to never initiate gossip, but then when others start gossiping you can't believe the words coming out of your mouth, the things you're agreeing with. It's easy to get sucked in. And it's hard to be the one who speaks up and brings gossip to a halt, but that's exactly the right thing to do.

Learn to quickly recognize a breach of integrity and stop it cold. Disrupt it. When I catch myself starting to gossip or say something negative, I quickly change the end of the sentence. Or I trail off with the comment "I forgot what I was going to say."

Women in any kind of career advancement, leadership or role model position, including motherhood, must absolutely avoid falling into the gossip trap. It belittles you, sends a negative message and detracts from your influence. Reclaiming your integrity, once it's compromised, is about as easy as unspreading butter. Here's a tip: You won't get sucked in if you surround yourself with people who have the integrity not to gossip.

I'm no saint, and like most women I need to vent my feelings, so I give myself permission to have one trusted person as my gossip buddy, my "second mom." Blanche's integrity is unquestionable. I feel totally free and secure talking with her about anything. Sharing a troublesome situation with this wise woman helps me clarify what happened and prevent repetition. I'll ask her, "How would you have handled this?" Then I try to turn the negative experience into a learning opportunity. Spiritual without being rigid or hypocritical, Blanche has the life lessons and a perspective from her 70s that can mentor me to make good decisions in my 50s.

DO THE RIGHT THING WHEN NO ONE IS LOOKING

The expression "action speaks louder than words" is never truer than in respect to integrity. Most of us can talk a good game, but what happens when we're alone, unobserved, and our integrity is tested?

Every day people surf the Internet on company time, blanking their screen when the boss shows up. They work a lot slower than they're capable of, persistently take longer breaks, arrive late or sneak out early without permission. Everybody does it, so what's the big deal?

One of my employees asked me, "How do I know if I've violated company policy?" I told him it was simple. "If you wouldn't do it with me standing beside you, then you know it's a violation." As Ann Richards said, "You can dress up a pig, put on lipstick and call her Monique. But it's still a pig." You don't have integrity if you only have it when someone else is looking.

Kelly, a young mother who has physical limitations, was grocery shopping one day. Along with her basketful of goods, she purchased a heavy case of formula. After reaching her car, buckling her baby into the car seat and unloading the groceries, she realized the clerk had not charged her for the case of product. Someone else might have thought, "Their mistake, my advantage. I'm tired, my leg hurts, I'm going home." Despite her discomfort, however, Kelly got out of her car, unloaded the heavy case, unloaded the baby, went back into the store and paid for the goods.

If she had not acted on her integrity, who would have known? She would. When we have a break with integrity, the biggest break is with ourselves. Integrity is not only the bedrock of your relationships, integrity is your strength. And like cracks in a foundation, every small compromise in your integrity weakens the structure of your life. You must invest integrity in every situation, even when there's no one to notice.

REFUSE TO BE AN INTEGRITY VICTIM

As the victim of another person's lapse of integrity, you feel violated and hurt. But you can learn from it. When this happens to me, I try to turn it into a lesson.

Two employees seriously breached our company's integrity standards, and I had no choice but to fire them. It hurt to discover that these two people I cared about were manipulating sales reports. After it was all over I asked myself, "Was there some integrity issue manifesting itself in me that led to this?" I didn't like asking the question, because I pride myself on my integrity. Although it hurt to turn that question inward, it was insightful. I considered areas in my personal and business life where I had yet to perfect integrity, and I vowed to do just that.

Sometimes breaches of integrity feel like personal assaults, which for me often come from competitors. The more successful I am, the more I become the target of vicious, personal attacks, amusingly by people who have never met me and certainly don't know me. I choose to laugh about how much energy they spend on me and my company. Our strategy is to shrug it off and refuse to engage in a counterattack. It's not that I pretend competitors and undeserved attacks don't exist, because they do, but I try not to base our actions on them. And when anyone repeats a tactless remark a competitor has made about us, I just say, "You might consider that the comment came from a competitor," and leave it at that.

Women often feel compelled to explain themselves too much. You want to look right, and in the process you make another person wrong and risk making yourself look even more wrong. I would rather let people judge me wrongfully than explain myself in a way that compromises my own integrity.

Any time we're falsely accused or others are making us the "bad guy," we can't help feeling the weight of it, even if they're totally wrong. However we remedy the situation, we have to ask ourselves, "Did I breach integrity in some way?" If so, own up to it. If not, then own up to that, too. Just because a faction differs with your opinion doesn't mean they're right or you're wrong. If you can remedy the problem without making anyone the bad guy, do so. If not, demonstrate your own integrity and be more concerned about who you are than who you are reputed to be. Be less dependent on praise, and criticism will sting a lot less.

AVOID THE LURE OF MANIPULATION

One of my friends, who is now divorced, told me she couldn't get her ex-husband to attend to any project around the house until she learned to manipulate his responses. He was handy enough to fix a window or repair a wall, and would do it—at some future time of his choosing. When she wanted a cabinet built for her kitchen, months passed and she still had inadequate storage space. Finally, she waited until he was at work, bought the materials and tackled the cabinet herself. When he came home, she was busily nailing boards together. He said, "That will never stand up. You're not doing it right." He took the tools from her and finished the cabinet. In the future, when she needed his attention on the house, she knew exactly how to get it.

Unfortunately, this positive outcome reinforced a negative concept: manipulation. It's only a small step from manipulating your spouse into doing those pesky tasks to using manipulation without integrity. When you start manipulating, you're on a slippery slope. Perhaps you manipulate acquaintances to wangle favors. Eventually you find yourself manipulating friends, spouses, children and coworkers. What happens to these relationships? Where are the trust and mutual respect? Then you gently manipulate sales figures to show more attractive results. The collapse of Enron is an example of manipulation and the correspondingly high cost of the lack of integrity. Avoid being lured into manipulation; it never leads to authentic success.

LIVE AUTHENTIC SUCCESS

Use these 11 strategies to attract the brightest opportunities that come from living a life of uncompromising integrity:

1. Live by the Golden Rule.

2. Be honest with yourself and make decisions as objectively as possible. If you're uncertain, seek the opinion of a trusted mentor.

3. Surround yourself with people who glow with integrity. Have you ever noticed what happens to a bag of apples when one apple goes bad? If you leave it in the bag, all the apples touching it will rot. Remove yourself from "bad apples."

4. Speak up when you see a breach of integrity. Silence can be as hurtful as words or actions. Cultivate dialogues for stating your honest opinion in uncomfortable situations. Write these down and memorize them for easy recall when an unexpected situation puts you on the spot.

5. Promote integrity by acknowledging the wise choices your friends and coworkers make.

6. Engage 100 percent. If you're an employee, put 100 percent effort into the job. As a friend, put 100 percent into your friendship. If you accept an opportunity, invest 100 percent effort in the outcome. Cut back on commitments and people to whom you're not willing to give 100 percent.

7. Keep your promises, to yourself and others, and follow through on commitments, even when delivering on the promise is difficult or when a more exciting opportunity presents itself.

8. Eliminate excuses. Don't allow commitments to your children or spouse, lack of time or the stress of your job to lead you down the path to compromise. Do whatever it takes to live up to your word. It's easier to keep promises you really want to make, so avoid committing too quickly and don't overcommit.

9. Admit when you're wrong. When I'm courageous enough to admit I'm wrong or I've made a mistake, I'm amazed at the generosity of the person on the receiving end. This increases trust, elevates credibility and strengthens the relationship.

10. Avoid mean and hurtful communication. Communicating with kindness always results in more positive impact. Reverse the tendency to make negative remarks by focusing on a person's best qualities. Say three nice things about someone you dislike.

11. Forgive your own transgressions. Just because we have a breach in integrity doesn't mean we're not allowed to move forward. A woman who had an affair confided, "Integrity is something you have to have all of the time and I don't have it all of the time, so I don't have it." Maybe she was right, but there comes a time to learn from our mistakes and move on.

Nobody is perfect. Show me one woman who has never transgressed, and I'll nominate her for sainthood. When you do or say what you know is wrong, rectify it. If you can't rectify it, at least learn from it. Then forgive everything about yourself and move on.

Practice Uncompromising Integrity with the
5 PROMISES

PROMISE 1

I Will Live and Work a Passionate Life

Is there an integrity issue (in you or someone else) that is preventing you from living your passionate vision? Describe it.

_____

_____

_____

PROMISE 2

I Will Go for It or Reject It Outright

How does this integrity issue impact your commitment to your passion?

_____

_____

_____

What can you do to soften that impact? Can you rectify a past misdeed? Is there someone to whom you need to apologize, have a long talk with or repay a debt? Is there someone you need to stand up to? If so, set a target date to handle the transgression, absolve the guilt or confront the problem and move on.

_____

_____

_____

*P*ROMISE 3

I Will Take One Action Step a Day Toward My Passionate Vision

Write down three ways you will practice uncompromising integrity. Beginning today, vow never to break this covenant with yourself.

---

*P*ROMISE 4

I Commit to Being a Success Student for Life

Write down the name of a person with uncompromising integrity who has something you want (more peace, more success, etc.). Study how she handles compromising situations and model her.

---

*P*ROMISE 5

I Believe as a Woman I Really Can Do Anything

Recall situations in which you demonstrated integrity, possibly when others did not. Write down as many as you can recall. Notice how you feel and write down your feelings.

Download the 5 Promises for Integrity at InsideEveryWoman.com.

JAN'S *Integrity*

I struggled through school and I don't do well on standardized tests, and my counselor made it quite clear that I wasn't college material. Talk about a breach of integrity! Couldn't he have looked more closely at my skills and found a way to encourage me?

Well, I had to prove him wrong. I completed college, became a teacher and obtained a master's degree. Teaching is my passion. I love kids. The pay isn't lucrative, but I love the work.

I also take special kids on field trips during the summer. The parents are usually excited about it, and with that trip I can make the extra money I need. These special kids have a wonderful summertime experience they might otherwise have missed, while the parents also get a much-needed break.

I often think about that counselor. If I had the chance I would tell him, "Thomas Edison's teacher foolishly thought he was addled. You can do your job with integrity and, at the same time, give kids a sense of value."

Jan, 52
Learning Specialist

As you practice uncompromising integrity to achieve success, learn how the next Feminine Force, endurance, can take you the extra mile in living your passionate vision.

> *Break one thread—through evil intent or casual carelessness,*
> *by deliberate action or mere inattention—*
> *and the whole fabric defining you will unravel.*
> —S. J. Rozan

I will not be vanquished.
—Rose Kennedy

Growth of any kind cannot occur without
enduring some degree of pain and discomfort.
—Vickie L. Milazzo

ENDURANCE

Fuel Your Endurance to
Energize Your Performance

In the 1924 Olympic Games 400-meter freestyle, the winning
time for women was 16 percent slower than for men. That endurance difference shrank to 11.6 percent in 1948 and then to
6.9 percent in 1988. The gap is closing in other sports, as well.
An exercise physiology expert suggests that the difference may be
more sociological than physiological—males have always trained
earlier and harder than females—and we may soon see women
outperforming men.

In general, women outlive men by an average of seven years.
Among centenarians, people 100 years or older, women outnum-
ber males four to one. That's endurance.

Many women who choose to become mothers endure 14 or
more hours of labor. That's 14 hours of pain. And while we might

assume that mothers-to-be have no idea what to expect the first time they're picking out tiny pastel onesies, most of them go back and do it again.

But endurance is about more than sports or longevity or pain. Endurance is a potent and positive strength we can use to push onward toward a vision that may seem so far in the distance we often wonder if our passion will hold out. Endurance is about having the inner strength to sustain commitments you make to yourself and others, even when you'd rather quit. How many women do you know who have gone back to school to obtain a higher degree even while working a full-time job and raising a family? Like Sharon, who decided to become a lawyer even though she hadn't finished college. In six nonstop years of night school, she did it. Women every day endure long hours of work, family responsibilities, study and sleep deprivation to eventually have a career and life that fulfills their vision.

One of my favorite endurance allegories is about an East African tribe that became famous for its rain dances. This tribe was unique in all of Africa because its rain dances always succeeded. Other tribes in the region had low or mediocre success rates, but this tribe alone was 100 percent successful.

Members of rival tribes jealously studied this phenomenon, theorizing that the tribe had better dancers, special steps, more powerful chants, or more sincere prayers, or that their costumes, feathered accoutrements and masks made the difference. Finally, they claimed it was simply luck that made the gods smile on that one fortunate tribe but not on their own.

After observing the tribe's practices, an anthropologist uncovered the secret to their 100 percent success rate. He was surprised that it was so simple. They had no special powers, no magical interventions. They simply danced their rain dance until it rained.

They never quit, never gave up and never grew despondent over how long it took for the rain to come. They expected it would always rain when they danced, and their experience supported their belief. They just kept dancing, knowing that sooner or later the gods would be satisfied and reward their persistence with rain. Rewarded they were—every single time.

This is one of the most basic and simple secrets to success. It's always easier to quit the dance but much more rewarding to dance on. All it takes is endurance.

KEEP DANCING YOUR PASSIONATE VISION

Endurance is also about having the emotional intelligence to wait for success. When I was young I wanted to change the world, and I wanted it to happen *now.* That unrealistic goal resulted in frustration until I learned to chill about the outcome. At times, the space between reaching for an objective and realizing it seems unendurable, but I endure the wait because I know the moment will arrive, and it will pass all too quickly.

Today I'm content with growing my business 15 percent each year; it doesn't have to double or triple. I'm content with helping one group of nurses at a time to a new level of success; I don't have to change the whole healthcare system. I keep myself plenty busy while enduring the space between desire and fulfillment. As a result, I'm not fighting my own frustration.

Have you ever watched a woman who has a background or talent similar to your own become successful while your efforts stalled? Have you ever coveted another person's success and rationalized why they were more successful than you? I've seen women succeed far beyond their dreams and watched others founder and give up. What distinguishes successful women from their less successful sisters?

Certainly it's easy to credit another's success to luck, money, connections or lack of children, yet famous women in a variety of pursuits prove that none of these is the essential success ingredient.

✦ Sarah Josepha Hale, known for her poem "Mary Had a Little Lamb," badgered six presidents and endured scores of negative responses over a 36-year period before she finally convinced Abraham Lincoln to proclaim Thanksgiving a national holiday.

✦ Born the 20th of 22 children, premature and stricken by a procession of childhood illnesses including polio, Wilma Glodean Rudolph endured to become the first American woman to win three Olympic gold medals.

✦ Determined to help her twice-widowed mother with the family finances, young Phoebe Ann Moses, later known as Annie Oakley, practiced with her father's old Kentucky rifle. By hunting small game and selling it to hotels and restaurants, she earned enough to pay off her mother's mortgage. She was 16 when she beat well-known marksman Frank Butler in a shooting contest.

✦ A year after being dragged from icy waters during her aborted first attempt to swim the English Channel, Gertrude Ederle plunged again into the water at Cape Gris-Nez in France. She was assailed by wind, rain and powerful currents in water brimming with stinging jellyfish and the occasional shark. She had already endured the humiliation of her previous defeat and ridicule from the press, which asserted that no female could swim the Channel. But having developed her "never quit" attitude as a child after a near-fatal drowning accident, Gertrude shattered the existing men's record by more than two hours. In fact, due to rough waters, she swam an extra 14 miles on top of the 21-mile crossing.

The big commonality for all of these women is endurance. They chose to keep dancing their passionate vision, with full expectation of reward.

When I first knocked on attorneys' doors, I knew they had a need and would hire me, so I kept knocking until they did. I kept dancing my passionate vision fully expecting to be rewarded.

FUEL YOUR ENDURANCE WITH PERSISTENCE

In February of the year I was getting married, on my birthday no less, I lost a six-figure client and the mainstay of my consulting business when a law firm dissolved. It didn't make for a terrific day. That evening Tom and I had planned to go out with friends to celebrate my birthday, but my heart wasn't in it. We opted instead for a dinner of popcorn and saw the movie *My Left Foot,* the story of Christy Brown, whose cerebral palsy confined him to a wheelchair. Christy overcame all odds to become a celebrated writer and painter—using only his left foot, the single part of his body he could control. I left the theater a different person, my own problems seeming minor in comparison. The following months I threw myself into reorganizing my business.

That year wasn't terrific, but I endured and kept working to make it better. I could have surrendered and gone back into traditional nursing, but instead I stuck to my passionate vision of teaching with no guarantee of where I would land. This year my company will make 200 times my income that year. Eight two-day seminars a year evolved into the industry's leading education institution. Dancing my vision paid off handsomely.

I thought I personified endurance until I met Mary. I'm used to being the instructor, but in all my classes I learn at least one new thing from my students. One day this teacher turned serious student when Mary taught me a lesson in endurance. She had attached a letter to her seminar registration stating that she was deaf and would require a "signer." My initial annoyance at this imposition and expense heightened when I learned that not one but two professional signers would be required, alternating every 15 minutes. The cost of meeting Mary's needs was three times more than the tuition she paid. Besides, how could a deaf woman hope to establish her own business as a legal nurse consultant?

The first day of the seminar, Mary's signers arrived early and militantly staked out three seats in the front of the room—not in the back, where I had hoped to seat them. Unused to sharing the stage, I was already out of sorts when Mary and her seeing-eye dog arrived and I learned she was not only deaf but legally blind, with thick glasses to augment her limited vision. I now had to compete for my other students' attention with a pair of sign language interpreters and a dog.

And for what? There was no way a deaf, blind nurse could analyze medical records well enough to get business from attorneys.

I started the day by trying to pretend they weren't there at all, even when the dog barked for no apparent reason and laughter rippled through the crowd. Isolated by her dog's watchful protection and oblivious to the racket, Mary paid close attention to my every word. I pasted on my best plastic smile and patted myself on the back for handling the distraction so heroically, until eventually I accepted that my inconvenience paled in comparison to hers. Swallowing my humiliation, I approached Mary during a break and asked what had attracted her to legal nurse consulting.

She said, "I was working on my own malpractice case. The attorney was so impressed with my help that he said he'd hire me if I took your course." *Gulp.* I was grateful she couldn't see the surprise, guilt and contrition parading across my face.

Mary admitted that the eyestrain of trying to follow the text and the signing sent her back to her hotel room each evening with a severe migraine, but she was determined to endure the training and pass the exam. Which she did.

Despite the overwhelming odds against her, Mary began her days with a smile and fueled her endurance with persistence, working harder than the other students and knowing that each day she endured brought her one step closer to her big goal of starting her own business as a Certified Legal Nurse Consultant. I was honored to sign her certification card.

We each have our own endurance challenges. Any time we feel overwhelmed or on the verge of defeat, every step can seem an enormous effort, every minor conflict an obstacle. Yet a small change or action can make a huge difference. One toe inches forward, then another, and before long we've taken a stride past the obstacle, a stride that we once thought would never happen. Endurance enables you to stand alone or with others and accomplish whatever you choose to take on.

FUEL ENDURANCE WITH INCREMENTAL PAYOFFS

At Hawaii Volcanoes National Park, I set out to hike a 14-mile trail. Although this walk was longer than I'm used to taking, I didn't see it as an overwhelming challenge. I consider myself to be in excellent physical condition.

The combination of a long hike and an excessively hot day, made worse by the uneven, hot volcanic terrain, turned out to be more difficult than I expected. Four miles into this sauna I thought seriously about turning back.

Fortunately, my pride and stubbornness pushed me to endure. At the end of the trail, my endurance was rewarded with a breathtaking view of the active volcano, an eerie yet awesomely beautiful sight like nothing I'd ever experienced.

It wasn't this final payoff, but the amazing small payoffs I received along the way that helped me endure. The uniqueness of each square inch of the black lava formation I crossed; abundant plant life in this seemingly barren area; incredible red flowers superimposed on the stark background; and, in the 12th mile, the most beautiful rainbow I've ever seen—I would have missed it all if I had quit. Although the hike was a humbling experience, I had the satisfaction of knowing I had endured to the final payoff.

Women are masters of endurance. We endure high-heeled shoes only to be rewarded with aching feet. We spend precious minutes every morning putting on makeup, only to endure taking it off again that night. As mothers, we endure smelly diapers and 3:00 a.m. feedings to enjoy cuddling that bundle of pure joy. We endure the hassles over homework to celebrate our child's first outstanding report card, and the next and the next, until the ultimate reward of a diploma. That endurance comes naturally.

When my student Marie shared her story of entrepreneurial endurance, it reminded me of my hiking experience, because she did not anticipate the many challenges and difficulties of starting a business. Along the way she often felt overwhelmed and questioned whether she could possibly turn her part-time venture into a profitable full-time business.

But she refused to quit or turn back. Finally, after much hard work, things seemed to come together. In her 14th month she grossed $17,000—an amount she couldn't have imagined earning two months earlier—and this promised to be only the first of many similar rewards. If she had turned back when she doubted herself, not only would she have failed to receive that first big payoff, she also would never have known what she was truly capable of accomplishing.

Many women who fail in reaching their goals simply turn back too soon. The path is long and the terrain is rough. Unforeseen obstacles crop up: a difficult assignment, a fierce new competitor. Stop and analyze your efforts to see if adjustments should be made, but don't give up on your passionate vision and life goals. Sooner or later small payoffs will brighten your path—a colleague becomes a friend, you receive acknowledgment for an achievement, a door opens to new opportunity.

When your endurance is tested and you're tempted to give up, remember this: You will miss not only the gold at the end of the rainbow, but also a wealth of other treats along the way. Whether you're hiking or building a business or striving for a promotion, the ultimate reward goes to those who endure even when the big reward is far away in the distance. Fuel your endurance by actively planning small incremental payoffs.

FUEL ENDURANCE WITH THE RIGHT FOCUS

Great athletes focus on making the next stroke, pitch or swing even better than the last, not on the stitch in their side. When I'm in a hot yoga class, which is 90 minutes in a 105-degree room, I endure by focusing on each posture and my breathing, not on the sweat running down my face. I know I'll feel phenomenal afterward, that's a given, but I also try to enjoy the practice itself. I do best when I visualize perfecting the posture while at the same time concentrating on the instructor's dialogue and the muscles that are doing the work. I also repeat to myself a mantra: "This is my time. This is my 90 minutes. This is for me."

The free diver swims hundreds of feet down and back again on one breath. Every movement, every thought uses up precious oxygen. Can you imagine her worrying about when she'll get her next breath of air? Even worrying about beating her competitor's time is a dangerous distraction. Instead, she's mindful only of the task at hand, concentrating on performance.

Actress Jane Froman related her experience after badly injuring her leg in an airplane crash. "For about four months, I just lay there, thinking not-too-pretty thoughts. Then, one day, I got to wondering. I wanted desperately to sing; still, I hadn't sung in so long that I wondered whether I could . . . so I just did! And it felt wonderful. People in the hospital thought I'd gone crazy—that the leg pains had worked up to my head—but that didn't matter. I could sing! Whatever else was wrong with me, the breath-bellows and the voice-box were sound, and that was all that counted." Nine months after her accident, through the right focus, Froman performed in a Broadway show.

Wilma Glodean Rudolph focused first on survival, then on getting fit, then on running, not on polio.

Annie Oakley focused on shooting straight and true, not on being poor.

Gertrude Ederle focused on swimming the English Channel, not on the perils awaiting her in the water.

Focus is the rocket fuel of endurance. Concentrate on the right focus, the one thing that matters, and shut your mental door on all the rest.

ENDURE FOR THE FUN OF IT

One of the biggest factors contributing to failure in any endeavor is the naive assumption that to be passionate and enjoy your work you have to enjoy every aspect of what you do. Countless otherwise savvy and intelligent women blithely expect success to make every day a glorious picnic. Then, when they come face to face with the inevitable ants, mosquitoes and rain showers, they run for shelter.

If you assume you should enjoy everything you do every day, you'll wind up massively disappointed. You'll constantly be thinking there's something better someplace else. Then, when you arrive at that someplace else with your impossibly high expectations, the vicious cycle starts anew, leaving you dissatisfied again—and wondering how it happened when you were following your bliss toward the "perfect" future.

M. Scott Peck, author of *The Road Less Traveled,* contends that life is hard but that actually recognizing this fact makes life a lot easier. If you broaden your concept of fun to include the hard stuff, life does become easier.

A lot of people ask me, "Vickie, do you like being on the road speaking or being at home?" Wherever I am is where I want to be. When I'm on the road, I love being on the road. When I'm at home, I love being at home. If I don't have fun wherever I am, I'm spending a substantial amount of time in the wrong mindset.

My parents taught me that fun was where I made it. I was their shy, quiet and serious child, and they made it their mission to help me "lighten up." They'd get up a game of touch football for the neighborhood kids or take us all out for hot chocolate and beignets. Fun was one piece of parental advice I took to heart.

It's inevitable that we'll enjoy some experiences more than others. Getting praised for your work is fantastic. Going on vacation is bliss. Making a difference is rewarding. And we savor these high notes. But not every moment of success is rewarding or fantastic or bliss.

In your business or career, you endure the word "no" over and over to get to one fabulous "yes." Your "no" might come from a sales prospect who doesn't want to buy, or from your supervisor, who is not buying your innovative idea. One of my students, Dale, uses fun to endure rejection. She says, "The thought of showing up at a prospect's office with my marketing materials in hand terrified me at first. Then I began having fun with it, inventing new ways to get past the gatekeepers. Now, the challenge of seeing how many prospects will actually talk to me is a fun game."

Whether you're cleaning a closet or working overtime, you have a choice about how you label that experience. Endurance is a choice. Fun is a choice. The more you broaden your concept of fun, the deeper your endurance for achieving ultimate success.

TAKE TO THE AIR LIKE A BUTTERFLY

My grandmother Pearl always called me her butterfly. I loved that she saw me as someone who was beautiful and special. What I didn't know is that she was also referring to the transformation I would go through to become the woman I am today.

As a butterfly emerges from its cocoon, it struggles and strains to free itself. The struggle is essential to strengthen the wings and shrink the body. Without such strain, the butterfly's wings would be weak, its distended body ungainly and it would never take to the air. Butterflies everywhere who endure this struggle are rewarded with the glorious adventure of flying from blossom to blossom.

We are all constantly emerging from our cocoons, struggling and straining to become free, strong, beautiful women. Growth of any kind cannot occur without enduring some pain and discomfort. Here's your choice: You can play it safe, avoid the pain of growing, and experience the narrow, earthbound existence of the lowly caterpillar. Or you can throw yourself fully into the struggle of living, pain and all, and enjoy the soaring freedom of the lofty butterfly.

Building muscle mass is another "no pain, no gain" experience. To build muscle mass you have to hurt. And you won't just hurt the first few times you do it. If you're training correctly, it hurts every time you work out. If you're not hurting, you're only pretending to be working out. Bear in mind that this hurt is what trainers refer to as a "good hurt," not the kind that causes injury; but it's uncomfortable all the same.

Have you ever observed a person working out halfheartedly? Be careful that you're not playing that pretend game with yourself. Real growth requires real effort and real endurance. Don't take the easy way out, telling yourself you'll reach your performance goal by a shortcut that skips the painful part of the journey. Each hurt, each struggle you endure transforms you. Shortchange yourself in the effort department and you not only deceive yourself but also deprive yourself of the opportunity to grow.

To grow and build your success "muscles" you have to be willing to endure "hurt" on a regular basis. Eventually those muscles will turn into wings that fly you passionately onward.

FUEL YOUR ENDURANCE WITH FIRE

Endurance comes easy when we're passionately interested in what we're doing. A ballet dancer endures excruciating practice workouts to become excellent, but the pain doesn't stop when she perfects her talent. While performing, she's so intently focused that she may not feel pain, but after she pulls off her ballet slippers her battered, bloody feet make her cringe. She endures because she's passionate about dancing.

My customer service manager has taken the word "manager" out of her title because she doesn't like managing at all. But because she helped create the department and is passionate about it functioning at its highest level, she's willing to endure the position until the right manager is found. That sort of dedication only results from an inner fire.

As I've mentioned, I'm passionate about travel. I love flying away to exotic locales, but have you ever noticed the inconveniences travelers endure to enjoy their passion? It starts with the preparation to be gone for several weeks, packing for all that time away, then enduring the body cavity search at airport security, uncomfortable seats and airline food on the 12-hour overnight flight to Tokyo, multiple connections to Kathmandu and even more lines at passport control—knowing that after you've fully relaxed you'll have to endure it all again backwards. An airplane is so unfriendly to your body parts you're ready to abandon them in the seat pocket in front of you. You start questioning, "Why am I doing this?" Finally you're in Nepal enduring lost or damaged luggage, inedible food and accommodations too rough even for Marines. Part of you is miserable, while another part is muttering, "I love this, I really do." But when you finally trek the Himalayas, you're ecstatic to see that those holy mountains reaching into the heavens are worth every moment of your endurance.

Fire and endurance, when tightly connected, can take you all the way to the top. My business is a good example. I passionately love entrepreneurship, but the employee and management issues are an endurance for me. Because I love the creative development of the business, and I enjoy the relationships that surround it, I endure the less desirable aspects.

I'm continuously amazed at the variety of businesses that people seem to be passionate about, especially those that make and sell only one type of widget. I couldn't wrap my passion around a widget, so I would never have the endurance to make such a business successful. I'm thankful that other people can get fired up about making widgets, because otherwise they would never get made. Likewise, I've seen people whose spectacular idea never gets off the ground because they don't have the passion to endure what's required.

Since I started writing this book, I can't count the number of people who've told me, "I plan to write a book some day." They have a bright idea for a book, and they think that's all it takes. But even the brightest idea doesn't shed any light until it's expressed in 70,000 words, or 280 manuscript pages. It means enduring days and weeks and even months of fleshing out your idea until you finally type "The End," and then enduring more weeks of revision upon revision. You need more than a bright idea; you need a passion for writing that makes endurance possible.

To reach the end of anything—a project, hike or 14 hours of labor—you need the Feminine Force of endurance. Fortunately, women have all the endurance they need. Merge endurance with your passion, and you can accomplish anything.

HARVEST ENERGY TO INCREASE YOUR ENDURANCE

Somewhere in your home you have an appliance, a clock or a laptop computer that runs on electricity but has a backup battery. Like that battery, endurance is there when you need it. But without occasional recharging, a battery runs out of power. So will you, if your energy is not fueled by passion, focus, fun or another renewal source.

One source you can count on for harvesting more energy is positive relationships. We all know at least one person who lifts our spirits and makes us feel more alive. It might be your mother, your spouse, a good friend, your children or, if you're truly fortunate, all of them. Surround yourself with positive relationships, especially with those who support your passionate vision, and your natural endurance will be eternally rechargeable.

If positive relationships can power up your endurance battery, what do you think happens when you invest time in negative relationships? *Zap!* Why squandor such a valuable resource? Don't tolerate a relationship that returns little or nothing despite how much you put into it. Limit any exposure to people who drain you, and sever dark, toxic relationships.

I love my employees, but I know my limitations when it comes to enduring employee issues. In my start-up days, I handled everything. Employees waited until the end of a long day to come into my office, shut the door and say, "I need to talk with you." Add issues such as coworker conflicts, bare midriffs, sick children, flu season, bad hair days and people crying on my desk—and that was just the men! Talk about a constant drain. Now I have the luxury of working at home a couple of days a week. I hired four directors on whom I can rely to run the day-to-day operations, and I interact with them by phone or e-mail. Women can find creative ways to endure, but when possible we should step away to recharge and improve performance.

Other energy zappers include the many types of mental and physical clutter we talked about in Chapter 2. People might think I've created my own little bubble world by cutting so much clutter out of my life, but I don't need to belong to six professional organizations, get involved with their committees and sit on the advisory boards. Yes, some people find that recharging; I find it draining.

Watch athletes on the tennis court or golf course. They're not chatting between rounds. They're harvesting energy for endurance. When you're mindful, you're not wasting energy. Masters of endurance are very good at blocking out the world. Life offers

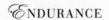

many opportunities to be involved, but with your energy all over the place how can you passionately pursue your vision? Energy is life. Energy is essential for endurance. Detach from all energy-draining obligations and people who do not align with your vision, and conserve your stamina for what matters.

10 STRATEGIES FOR BUILDING YOUR ENDURANCE MUSCLES

Endurance is a strength you can build by working out. Muscling up your inner power to match your passion is no different from building larger, stronger biceps. It takes focus, dedication and discipline. If you stop going to the gym, your muscles atrophy. If you stop strengthening endurance, you lose it.

1. *Energize your vision.* Do whatever it takes to make your intuitive vision as real as if it has already taken form. Use sight, sound, smell, taste and touch to keep the dream alive so it is vivid and real when the test of endurance comes. One woman in our office has a CD of soothing ocean sounds she plays during her daily breaks. Your inspiration might be a recorded song or instrumental. It might be sounds of nature or a movie soundtrack. Or it might be a photo of a lake, a stairway in your dream house or a sharp-looking business suit. Pin a colorful collage of inspiring symbols where you can see it as you work.

2. *See the light.* Endurance comes easier when you can see the light at the end of the tunnel, when you know what you must endure and for how long. Make a plan.

3. *Power up with knowledge.* Fuel yourself with all the skills and information you need, and also with any peripheral

knowledge that might give you an edge. Knowledge makes endurance less of a struggle.

4. ***Engage assistance.*** It takes a relay of runners to carry the Olympic torch all the way around the world. Who can you engage to make your burden lighter or your journey easier?

5. ***Practice.*** Some things you have to experience to endure. When I first started teaching, I taught all day. At first it was hard; now it's easy.

6. ***Take an endurance break.*** When you work out with weights, you shouldn't exercise the same muscles two days in a row. Similarly, give yourself an occasional break from your ordinary world. Do something totally different, see different sights, meet new people, experience a ballet or opera. Go to a bookstore and spend an afternoon visiting a new world. Rent travel DVDs, then order food and play music from that exotic locale. Immerse yourself. Avoid answering the phone or otherwise getting drawn back into your real world. You'll feel stronger when you return.

7. ***Break the marathon.*** When you're running an endurance marathon, taking five-minute breaks every hour gives you renewed energy for endurance.

8. ***Acknowledge your successes.*** Acknowledging what you've endured in the past strengthens your endurance for the next challenge.

9. ***Take care of yourself.*** A healthy body, mind and spirit fuel endurance.

10. ***Think straight.*** Your thoughts control your life, and as your most intimate companions, your thoughts can help you endure. Don't dwell on the competition. Don't dwell on the problem. Focus on the solution and the task at hand.

Fuel Your Endurance with the
5 *P*ROMISES

*P*ROMISE 1

I Will Live and Work a Passionate Life

What do you find most difficult to endure (mentally, physically, etc.) in pursuing your passionate vision?

_____

_____

_____

*P*ROMISE 2

I Will Go for It or Reject It Outright

What meaningful sounds and sights lift your spirits and strengthen your endurance? Write them down, then revisit this collection daily.

_____

_____

_____

Do you associate with anyone who belittles you, depresses you or otherwise zaps your energy? If so, how will you detach from this person?

_____

_____

_____

$\mathscr{P}$ROMISE 3

I Will Take One Action Step a Day Toward
My Passionate Vision

What three action steps will you take to strengthen the area of endurance identified in Promise 1?

_____

_____

_____

$\mathscr{P}$ROMISE 4

I Commit to Being a Success Student for Life

Name a woman who exemplifies endurance for you. How will you model her success to fuel your endurance?

_____

_____

_____

$\mathscr{P}$ROMISE 5

I Believe as a Woman I Really Can Do Anything

What challenges have you met that required endurance? How will you use those successes to strengthen your endurance in the future?

_____

_____

_____

Download the 5 Promises for Endurance at InsideEveryWoman.com.

SUSAN'S ENDURANCE

I trained for a year for the Houston marathon. Then about a month before the marathon I decided there wasn't any way I could do 26 miles. After a particularly hard training run at 18 miles, I did not believe I could do much more. The person helping me said, "Oh, yes you can." I kept going, kept training. The whole time I was telling myself, "You can do this, you can do this." When I got to the point in the marathon where other people hit the wall—the 20-mile mark—I kept telling myself, "Only 6 miles to go. You do more than that each day in training. It's no big deal." I did it, and it was a fabulous experience.

The endurance of running the marathon was nothing compared to the endurance of breast cancer. There's an enormous mind game you play with yourself, hearing the news that you have breast cancer and deciding what you are going to do with that information. Thinking positively, and seeing the light at the end of the tunnel, I carried on. What I learned from the experience was to trust God's plan above all and to know that we are never ever given more than we can endure. I also learned to test myself and push the envelope, to know that my mind is a powerful tool.

I wrote down a quote that has inspired me over time: "Expand what you know you can do." Certainly my experience with cancer helped me to do that.

Constantly talking to yourself, reassuring yourself—to me that's how endurance is sustained. That's what helped me through chemo and the bad days and reminded me I had something to look forward to. Now I've been cancer-free for six years, and while I'll never run another marathon, I'm learning every day how much more I can do.

Susan, 55
Interior Designer

Knowing you have the Feminine Force of endurance to sustain your passion, let's explore how endurance can be less of a struggle when coupled with the next strength, enterprise.

Nothing contributes so much to tranquilize the mind as a steady purpose—
a point on which the soul may fix its intellectual eye.
—Mary Wollstonecraft Shelley

*Find out what you like doing best and
get someone to pay you for doing it.*
—Katherine Whitehorn

*Enterprise is in a woman's DNA—
just look at what we accomplish.*
—Vickie L. Milazzo

ENTERPRISE

Become the CEO of Your Career and Life

As a child, did you ever "pioneer" an idea? Are you a self-starter? Did you ever sell cookies, greeting cards or lemonade? If so, perhaps you're an entrepreneur at heart. Many women are. Women in this country own more than 15.6 million businesses and generate trillions of dollars a year in business revenues. Between 1997 and 2004 the growth rate of women-owned businesses was twice that of all companies combined.

Women understand enterprise. Whether you choose to use your enterprising strength to start a venture of your own, manage your family or build a corporate career, enterprise is already inside you.

My grandfather and grandmother owned a neighborhood grocery store, and they worked equally hard, but she was the driving force behind the enterprise. Women have traditionally managed the household, the family and usually the household budget. They handle everything from first aid to food preparation, from car pool to caretaking. Effectively doing it all involves enterprise.

On trips to Thailand and Vietnam, I encountered woman's enterprising spirit at its rawest and liveliest. Everywhere I looked women were running businesses. They hawked new clothing, used clothing, lemonade in plastic baggies and everything else you can imagine, including cobras inside bottles of liquor. Women weighing 95 pounds carried yokes with complete soup kitchens balanced upon them: bowls, utensils and food on one side, a charcoal grill holding pots of broth and tea on the other. The grill was hot, and the pots simmered even as the women walked. In Southeast Asia fast food comes to you.

Enterprise can be any undertaking of adventure and initiative, and the reward doesn't have to appear in the form of a paycheck or dollars in the bank. You can employ enterprise to be the CEO of your life, for when you think about it, life is the biggest enterprise of all. Enterprise is a strength. Apply it to any desired goal, including the pursuit of your passionate vision.

But there does need to be a payout. What ultimate reward will come from living your passionate vision? Whether you want to make a difference, own a Porsche or both, get emotionally in touch with that payoff and let it inspire you. If you're already an entrepreneur or engaged in any passionate enterprise, reaffirm all the reasons you started your venture. To excel at enterprise, a CEO keeps her vision in sharp focus.

BE FIRST AT THE RIVER TO GET A DRINK

During a photo safari on Tanzania's Serengeti Plain, I encountered the least enterprising animal on earth, the wildebeest. I sat on a riverbank for three hours watching a herd of thousands build up the courage to drink from the water. This herd was part of the Great Migration that happens like clockwork every summer. More than a million wildebeests travel northward from the arid Serengeti into the wetlands of Kenya's Masai Mara, a long, dry and arduous journey. Frequently, the only available water is the Grumeti River, which represents both life and death. Unlike some creatures that can take moisture from the grass they eat, wildebeests must drink from the river to live.

The river supports other wildlife, including predators. Crocodiles may lurk just beneath the surface. Though thirsty from traveling, the wildebeests stand back from the water, sensing potential danger.

Inching toward the bank can take hours, as an individual wildebeest steps forward tentatively, sniffs the air, makes the plaintive "gnu" sound, steps back and then cautiously steps forward again. The herd bunches together and advances, gradually nudging the leaders to the river, whether they want to go or not. It's been a long time since they last drank, and you feel their desperation.

Lions, lazy creatures but possibly the most enterprising of all, are potentially on the watch, conserving energy as they await an opportunity for lunch. Once the herd stretches to the river, the lions could charge, trapping a wildebeest and stampeding the others. The frantic rush would raise a dust cloud that obscures the view of the wildebeests nearby. A kill is almost guaranteed.

The day I sat on that riverbank, a young wildebeest finally stepped ahead of the herd and drank while the fearful adults held back. Soon, others began drinking. But instead of lining up along the bank, taking turns, they bunched together fearfully and pushed until the surging masses shoved one wildebeest farther into the water than it was willing to go. It panicked and in turn panicked the others. They all retreated hastily and returned to the migration. Only the few brave enough to test the leading edge got a drink. The others went thirsty.

There was no danger from predators that day. Only the wildebeests' fear and lack of enterprise kept them from drinking.

The wildebeests reminded me of my fellow nurses when I worked at the hospital. They would bunch up at the water cooler airing their dissatisfaction with the work environment, but they never acted to end their desperation. Complaining was easier.

I decided I would no longer stand at the water cooler waiting for a drink. From the beginning, I treated my venture not as a part-time hobby but as an opportunity to quench my thirst for a more exciting and rewarding career. Refusing to hang out with the wildebeests and get eaten up by the lions, I became the CEO of my life.

You can, too. Enterprise is the ability to spot an opportunity and apply calculated action to receive a payoff. The lions' enterprising nature enables them to take on a herd of thousands of wildebeests. Their payoff is lunch. No doubt you've successfully managed many tough situations and, like the lion, have enterprise already inside you. Engage that enterprise to drink deeply of your passionate vision.

SATISFY YOUR THIRST AT THE RIVER OF CHOICE

While every woman is enterprising, not every woman is entrepreneurial. As an entrepreneur, I'm grateful for those enterprising women who work for me. They share many of my strengths and possess unique strengths of their own yet have no desire to start their own businesses. They prefer working as a team, possibly taking on leadership roles or interfacing at the front line with customers.

Only you know which river of success fits your personality and passionate vision. As the CEO of your life you must also be the CEO of your career. Let's say you work in a regional division of a national import company. Your department handles household furnishings and accessories. You can advance in two ways: by forging a path through the corporate maze or by striking out on your own as an entrepreneur.

The Corporate Formula

Do you like working with a team and with systems designed by others? Is your idea of security a steady paycheck with guaranteed benefits? Then the corporate route is for you. To forge your corporate path, research the top levels of your division to identify positions that match your passionate vision, and explore other divisions for jobs of interest. Next, plot a course from that lofty position you aspire to attain back to where you are now, pinpointing one or more positions at every level that will lead to your ideal career. Keep your vision bold, without concern for obstacles.

Study the people who currently hold those positions. How did they get to where they are? Did they rise from within the company or come on board at their current level? If possible, get to know them personally. People advance because of relationships, so build relationships at all levels. Be friendly with everyone, but remember that advancement comes from the top down and a little sucking up never hurts. Never sabotage managers or coworkers. You'll need them.

Align yourself with the company and make your goals consistent with the company's goals. Make work fun and engage 100 percent. Clock-watchers who go home exactly at quitting time are never around for promotions, or for the fun. Work as hard as or harder than your boss. If you're the supervisor, work as hard as your employees and as smart as your upper management.

Rather than looking only at your advancement, look for ways in which your skills and know-how can benefit the company. As a business owner, I appreciate employees who apply enterprise and ingenuity to their jobs. They generally enjoy their jobs more and receive more advancements and pay raises.

For years I trusted only Tom to handle the multimedia show at my seminars. Then one employee demonstrated the desire and skill to take on that job. It was a leap of faith for me to let him do it, because my performance depends a great deal on the person running the multimedia. This wasn't even an advancement for him, just an additional responsibility, but he was totally energized by this new facet of his career. Meanwhile, he was showing us that he's capable of doing more than his job description.

Another employee in our company has never asked for a pay raise but gets them because she throws her energy into every project. She wants to advance the company. In turn, I want to advance her. Demonstrate your desire to use all your strengths in the advancement of your company or department.

Investigate any new skills you need and learn them. Some skills are developed through education, others through experience. Many of the skills I have now, including the ability to manage business issues, conduct seminars and publish books and DVDs, came through experience. My business is a big laboratory, and every day is an experiment. On some days we invent new creations; on others we're sweeping up broken beakers. Open up, experience, experiment and learn.

Cut the excuses. Never assume that any lack (education, skill or ability) will hold you back. As an enterprising CEO, you maneuver past such obstacles. Communicate your strengths, not your weaknesses. If you're not advancing, ask yourself why. If you can't find the answers within, ask your supervisor, "Can you tell me three things I need to do to advance to the next level?"

Be patient. A common interview question is "Where do you see yourself in five years?" Nobody says, "In this exact same place," but the reality is that you might be in the same position for several years before advancing. You have to be willing to pay your dues. On the other hand, if your company clearly has no place for you to advance, move on.

The Entrepreneurial Formula

Are you the rebel—mouthy and opinionated? Do you like the thrill of change? Are you always eager for the next new venture? Is your idea of security to never be the victim of a corporation's downsizing or reengineering? Are you a fiercely independent risk taker who can comfortably handle the uncertainty of being responsible for your own paycheck? If the answer is yes, then the entrepreneurial route is right for you.

If you choose the entrepreneurial route, research your industry to identify types of businesses that match your passionate vision and aptitude. Explore areas that show growth potential and, using your experience and insight, look for a need not presently being filled. Then find a successful company similar to the one you envision owning, study how it started and how it grew and learn as much as possible about the entrepreneur behind it. Devour books and publications related to your business concept. Talk to other entrepreneurs to discover their best practices.

As an entrepreneur-in-training, you'll need to build both basic and advanced leadership skills. A successful entrepreneur is a bold visionary, seeing what others cannot and willing to follow that vision despite naysayers. Many entrepreneurs never finished college, but that hasn't stopped them from owning large companies like Dell and small companies like neighborhood restaurants and consulting firms. They relied heavily on their vision, not on MBA programs.

Entrepreneurs handle ambiguity with ease, get a thrill out of leading the way into unfamiliar territory and thumb their noses at failure. Fearless pacesetters, they are usually mystified to find that they are weak at operations and management. That's okay. Other people can manage for you, but you must be the guiding force that inspires your managers and staff to follow your vision. You'll shoulder responsibility and hold yourself personally accountable for the outcome. As a leader you have to focus on the big picture and trust others to focus on the details. People who do it all are self-employed but not entrepreneurial.

You must also be an actor. You act and get things done by delegating, subcontracting and leveraging other people's talents. You're innovative and unflaggingly determined, willing to put in fast-moving 16-hour days to reap the rewards of independence, creative freedom and unlimited financial gain.

Learn to be a marketing genius. You sell ideas to potential purchasers by getting inside their minds, creatively communicating the benefits they will receive when they buy in to your idea.

Above all, you must grow your enterprise and make a profit. People who say "I love it so much I'd do it for free" are not entrepreneurs—they're volunteers. Most entrepreneurs are willing to start small and grow slowly, but they fully expect to make money. There is nothing noble about being poor or failing financially.

Whichever route you choose, the corporate ladder or your own ladder, your success will be assured if you apply all 10 of your Feminine Forces to your enterprise.

Apply My Can't-Fail Enterprise Model

Whether you start a business, build a corporate career or focus your enterprising nature on a hobby or a family goal, my enterprise model guarantees success. Based on my CEO experience, you must do three things:

1. Construct a solid foundation.
2. Assemble an extraordinary framework.
3. Act like a CEO.

VENTURE OUT FROM A SOLID FOUNDATION

As you know, I started my business in my small condo. I worked solo. Every morning I hauled out my files and modest equipment and turned my home into a work space. Every evening I packed it all away again to make room for eating, sleeping and my personal life, what little there was of it. Within those modest surroundings I constructed a foundation for my enterprise. Today the Institute's foundation is not a room in my condo but 8,400 square feet of office space supported by a terrific team of enterprising staffers.

The foundation you build today will support your corporate career or entrepreneurial enterprise as you drive onward and upward. How do you make your foundation solid—indestructible, unshakable and enduring? Two ways: by starting with a Strategic Life Plan and commanding financial control.

Fortify Your Enterprise with a Strategic Life Plan

Consider the Golden Gate Bridge, the Brooklyn Bridge or London's Tower Bridge. How did the architects dare to create such astonishing visions? They didn't just look out at the future location, point a finger and say, "Pour the concrete right about there." Of course not.

Yet how often do we look out at the perilous waters of life, point a finger and say, "I'll just pour some concrete right there?"

An architect knows that failing to plan is planning to fail. Your life is more precious than any monument. Couldn't it also benefit from a blueprint to guide you?

As CEO, you need a Strategic Life Plan that projects your passionate vision. Whether loose or detailed, your plan should describe your vision and include the goals, or Big Things, you defined in Chapter 3, plus strategies and target dates. This is your blueprint for building your bridge to astonishing success.

My first strategic plan was conceived in my mind but only came fully to life when I committed it to paper. That single page included my goals and the strategies to achieve them, with a target date attached to each one. Every time I made a business decision, I consulted my plan. I reviewed and updated it frequently. It became my friendly nudge, my board of directors and my business manager. Today my company's strategic plan is 83 pages, because this level of planning is necessary to run my company, but it started with a simple page you can complete right now.

Envision a Bold Enterprise

If anyone had asked me 24 years ago whether I could manage a multimillion-dollar company, I would have laughed. My vision was smaller then. But that smaller vision got me to the bigger vision today. Don't hesitate to commit a plan to paper because it seems daunting; just start small. Starting small is better than not starting at all. Begin your plan by focusing on the passionate vision you developed in Chapters 1 and 2.

Describe the corporate, entrepreneurial or personal enterprise you will undertake to live this vision, and answer the question "What will this venture do for me?"

_____

_____

_____

Anchor Your Enterprise

The stability of your foundation comes from three cornerstones of balance: your values, your strengths and the way you handle challenges. Reconnect with your passionate vision while you identify these points.

1. *Define your core values.* This is not difficult, but it's somewhat magical, because your values will guide your decisions like a sage whispering in your ear. Every value should be deeply felt and embraced by your enterprise team. One of my company's core values is building lifelong relationships with our clients. My personal core values include commitment, integrity, excellence, fun and loyalty.

    Your values will shape your future as they have previously influenced your past and will help you design your Strategic Life Plan. *Write them down.*

    _____

    _____

    _____

2. *Assess your strengths.* You already possess knowledge, skills and experience your enterprise will draw on. One of my strengths is that I'm persistent and go for it all the way. *List all your strengths that apply to your enterprise.*

    _____

    _____

    _____

3. *Appraise your challenges.* Whatever your enterprise, you'll have challenges. These may involve market penetration, profitability, expertise, competition or getting along with your supervisor. Challenges change as your enterprise changes. My first challenge was getting clients to recognize the need for a new type of consulting service. When my company grew, a new challenge surfaced: my weakness as a manager. Without addressing that weakness, I might have worked solo forever, never achieving the bigger vision I could clearly see. That challenge led me to seek the right directors to support my vision.

> *What challenges will you face in pursuing your enterprise? How will they impact your goals and strategies?*

_____

_____

_____

_____

Shape Your Enterprise

Imagine your enterprise as it exists in your ideal future. Think large as you review the Big Things and action steps you wrote in Chapter 3.

1. Does your Big Thing match your enterprise or some part of your enterprise? If not, choose a Big Thing that does match your enterprise. Write this Big Thing on the "Goal/Big Thing" line on the Strategic Life Plan form on the next page.

2. What strategies will you use to accomplish your Big Thing? Do these match the action steps you wrote in Chapter 3? Develop your strategies and write them on your Plan form.

3. Add target dates for completion.

4. Repeat this process for all the Big Things you'll do to make your enterprise a reality.

STRATEGIC LIFE PLAN

VISION

_____

GOAL/BIG THING

_____

_____

STRATEGIES   **TARGET DATES**

1. _____   _____

     _____

2. _____   _____

     _____

3. _____   _____

     _____

4. _____   _____

     _____

5. _____   _____

     _____

Download a copy of this form at InsideEveryWoman.com for each Big Thing.

Finally, your Strategic Life Plan is only useful if it advances your passionate vision, and that starts with action. As the CEO of your life, you should constantly assess where you are in your Plan, what you have accomplished and which action step you'll take next. Your Plan is a practical document, not a theoretical one. It's a living organism you will use and update to live big.

Supported by your Plan and using your 10 Feminine Forces, you're ready for the next layer in structuring your foundation, financial control.

Command Financial Control in Your Enterprise

A competitor once commented sarcastically that my clients pay for my big house, my big vacations and my big smile. Of course they do. An enterprise is profitable or it isn't an enterprise—it's a charity. The word *profit* stems from the Latin word *profectus*, which means "advancement or improvement." Women should profit from their advancement. Even a nonprofit venture must have some profit to survive.

As CEO of your life, you deserve to achieve your desired level of financial growth. When I researched my first business idea for a patient education company, I was naively ready to go for it until I realized the enterprise wouldn't even support my lifestyle, which at that time amounted to $28,000 a year. I had to refocus my vision on an enterprise that could feed and shelter me.

Money to start, maintain and advance your enterprise is part of any sensible plan. Even carving your niche within a corporate structure may require an investment in education or training. But don't rush to your bank for a loan before seriously examining what you already have and what you'll need.

I started my business without one scrap of outside financial support. I had $100 in my savings account and a mortgage on my one-bedroom condo that required me to work overtime to pay. I was single, with no financial safety nets. I didn't even own a typewriter to type my reports. What I did have were all of the Feminine Forces we're discussing in this book.

Look first to your personal resources: savings, loans or family. For many ideas you won't need outside financing if you start small and grow your idea a little every day. Having no loan to repay is an asset. However, replacing frivolous purchases at the mall with a small monthly loan payment that could change your career, and ultimately your life, would be a wise investment. I know women who have built half-million-dollar consulting practices starting with $6,000 loans.

If part of your passionate vision is to be financially independent in your own business, try my method. Your clients provide your financing as you make money and invest your profits back into the enterprise. I started with one client, then gained a second and a third. I continued to work full-time as a nurse for 15 months while I built my part-time consulting practice. It was a challenge, running the business at night and on my days off, but I knew that if I was willing to bust my butt for a short time, I wouldn't be busting it for the next 35 years in the hospital.

Needing less is always a financial asset. Do you know people who can't finance a vacation, much less their passionate vision, because they want, want, want? Nothing will sabotage your enterprise more than financial worries. Freedom from such worries enables you to make forthright decisions. A CEO strategy for commanding financial control is to live beneath your income. While I encourage stretching way out when choosing goals, I don't believe that overspending is a solution to achievement.

Operating from my 1,100-square-foot condo until my business was extremely profitable and bringing in $1.2 million a year freed me to grow my business without the stress of high overhead. Acquisitions rarely satisfy for long, and when you're focused on your passionate vision you'll have less time for shopping.

Apply CEO financial management tools to your enterprise:

✦ Create an income and spending plan. Know where your money is going and question every expenditure.

✦ Once you have substantial income, create a monthly income statement and a balance sheet to monitor the financial health and well-being of your enterprise.

✦ Keep your new enterprise money separate from family money. This is a business, not a hobby.

✦ Keep the cash flow positive. That means taking in more money than you pay out, plain and simple. Make a budget and stick to it.

When you're confident that your enterprise can support itself and eventually become profitable, focus on the second part of the enterprise model—the framework.

ASSEMBLE AN EXTRAORDINARY FRAMEWORK

I could not imagine running the company I have now without the extraordinary framework of the staff, subcontractors, vendors and consultants who support it. In the early days, I didn't need that, nor would I have known what to do with it. Beginning with my first project, though, I knew I wanted to incorporate other talented people in my vision. I subcontracted with a typist, Rosa Lee, who had eight kids, and I taught them all how to support me in my home office.

Even if you work solo, you can benefit from a myriad of talented consultants, vendors and subcontractors. From day one I hired a subcontractor to assist me with client projects, which worked so well that I put off hiring my first employee for 10 years. Eventually I recognized that to stretch toward a bigger vision, I had to add employees to the framework. Expect your framework to change as your vision changes and grows. Build it only as big as you need.

People might think I go after all kinds of ideas, and I'll admit to constantly aiming for higher levels, but over the years I've rejected many ideas in my business. One idea I rejected was a division for locating expert witnesses for attorneys. I have thousands of contacts nationally, so creating this division would be easy and would add considerably to my bottom line, but I wouldn't enjoy it, so I don't do it.

Successful women can be successful at many things. Even though we all have to do things that aren't our top favorites, success lies in selecting and focusing on the things you like to do and do well.

If you've chosen the corporate route, create as many connections as you can with vendors, clients and professional peers. They will be your framework for your climb up the corporate ladder.

ACT LIKE A CEO

Not every enterprising woman wants to run a business, yet in many ways you already do. In life you're in charge of growth, finance, research and development, transportation, commissary, public relations, entertainment, maintenance and janitorial detail. If you're running a household while pursuing a career, you're responsible for all that and more. You're already a CEO, so why not act like one?

Whether your enterprise is career or family oriented or entrepreneurial, here are 13 secrets you can use.

1. *Everything is marketing.* As an enterprising woman, you
   know that getting a promotion or pay raise means selling
   your supervisor on your abilities, attitude and experience.
   That's marketing. When I received my master's degree in
   nursing, I knew I was a more valuable asset to the hospital,
   and I attempted to market that idea. They didn't buy in, so
   I marketed that same concept to a different hospital and got
   the raise I deserved.

   Perhaps your passionate vision doesn't include career or financial goals. Perhaps your vision is to bring together a widely
   separated extended family for a big reunion. The concepts
   of marketing still apply. You have to sell your reunion idea,
   including the date and place, to all family members.

   The simple concept behind marketing is this: Find a need,
   fill it and get people to buy in. Payoff is a two-way street.

   ✦ *What need will you fill?* A woman seeking promotion spots
     an opportunity to use her skills and experience in an area
     that will benefit the company or department she works for.
     An entrepreneur spots a need for products or services in
     her industry that is not adequately being met.

   ✦ *How will you fill it?* The corporate woman must have
     experience and knowledge that benefit her company. The
     entrepreneur must provide products or services to fulfill a
     need in the marketplace.

   ✦ *Who will buy it?* The corporate woman must sell her
     promotion to her supervisor who must then sell it to the
     management team. The entrepreneur must identify and
     understand her market to sell her products or services.

2. *Be your own number one fan.* Announce your achievements. This is hard for many women, but if you don't do it, who will? With humility, let people know when you've won an award, finished a big project, expanded your services or have an upcoming speaking engagement. Keep your name in front of everyone—your supervisor, your banker, your grocer. You never know where opportunity will strike.

   Announcing your achievements also validates the choices people have made on your behalf. The boss who promoted you, or the buyer who purchased from you, wants to know they bet on a winner.

3. *Expect icebergs.* No enterprise is unsinkable; the Titanic sank its first time out. But when your enterprise has a solid foundation and an extraordinary framework, and when you act like a CEO, only an enormous iceberg can knock you off course.

   In 1990 I hit an iceberg when my largest clients dissolved their law firm. Thankfully, I had the necessary lifeboats in place. My business stayed afloat and took a new course that changed my future and the nursing profession forever. If I had missed the iceberg, I might have continued in my original direction, satisfied with my solo consulting practice. And you'd be reading someone else's book.

   You have to sail before you can fail. You can maneuver around icebergs. But if you never leave the dock, you'll never have an enterprise to keep afloat.

4. *Solve problems quickly and decisively.* To become an enterprising problem solver, use the genius strategies in Chapter 5. Then apply the following eight-step system and use hypnagogic imagery before you fall asleep to arrive at inventive solutions. When you awake the solution will be waiting for you. You'll never be daunted by problems again.

8 STEPS TO
$\mathscr{F}$AST PROBLEM SOLVING

1. My problem is:

_____

2. It is important to me because:

_____

3. Current factors impacting and relevant to the
problem include:

_____

4. My overall goal in solving this problem is:

_____

5. The strategies I've already implemented to resolve
this problem include:

_____

6. People (family, consultants, housekeeper/nanny)
who can help me resolve this problem are:

_____

7. Actions I will personally take in the future include:

_____

8. Actions I will delegate include:

_____

Download this Problem-Solving tool at InsideEveryWoman.com.

5. *Listen.* Listening is an underutilized enterprise strategy. When we listen, we connect. We feel another person's energy, and they sense our interest. When selling an idea, listening is more effective than bombarding a person with information. People don't like to feel manipulated. When listening, don't interrupt. I have to work on this because I'm a fast thinker and I grew up in an Italian family where everyone talks at once, and to my husband's surprise, we're all listening, too.

6. *Don't be a commodity.* When you build relationships, you can never be duplicated. My company sells an educational experience. We don't sell seminars, DVDs or CDs, although those are the media we employ. Instead, we sell a relationship that includes mentoring. Our ideas might be duplicated, but our relationships with our customers cannot. If you're advancing through the corporate route, get in the middle of everything. Be involved. Don't shrink into your chair and become the invisible employee. Strive to stand out and demonstrate your ability to bring new ideas to a project or your workplace.

7. *Don't underprice yourself.* For 24 years people have said my products are too expensive—until they purchase and use them. Smart buyers understand that anything cheap can be expensive in the long run and will buy in to your enterprise as long as you provide value for the dollar.

   As an employee, make yourself valuable and hard to replace by building relationships throughout the company. Stamp your performance with originality so that you are not easily duplicated by a cheaper hire.

8. *Don't overrate networking.* Enterprising people are selective. I built my business on selective networking, but not through networking clubs. Such clubs can absorb time while distracting you from your Big Things. And you could be taking advice

from people who mean well but are not qualified to give it, so always assess the validity of advice offered.

9. *Invest in win-win relationships.* Enterprising women make sure they're not the only ones gaining from the initiative. Align with clients while also aligning with your support team of subcontractors, vendors and employees. Focus on what's in it for everyone. Create strategic alliances with people who can advance your career, and you theirs.

In the corporate world, it never pays to alienate a person who holds the cards. Treat everyone as an ally, even those who can't advance you. Have no enemies, never be condescending and practice integrity with everyone at every level. Avoid whiners, complainers and the wrong crowd. Although the wrong crowd might be the most popular, it won't be popular among the people who count.

10. *Compete only with yourself.* Mushing a dog sled across an Alaskan glacier, I learned firsthand that it's true—if you're not the lead dog, the view from the rear never changes. And the rear is exactly where you'll be if you compete only with others. To excel in enterprise you want to be aware of competition, but don't allow that awareness to veer you off course. Compete with your own best performance, be the lead dog your competitors imitate, and you'll leave them in the rear.

11. *Get your hands dirty.* I always joke that I'm a working CEO, a style that makes things happen. Successful CEOs get their hands dirty. All great chefs still work in the kitchen. You can't cook from behind your desk. Chop some onions.

12. *Make perpetual lists.* CEOs have assistants to remind them what to do. Like executive assistants, lists can save you hours of fumbling and head-scratching. Lists keep you organized and prevent wasted time going back for an item you forgot.

I keep a perpetual grocery list on my computer, which I simply update and print out when it's time to shop. I keep a list of travel items to pack no matter where I'm going. I also keep a list of future business ideas so I won't forget them. Which of your routines would benefit from being perpetualized on a grab-it-and-go list?

13. *Put systems to work for you.* CEOs like to spend their time creating, so they're adept at systemizing routine tasks. Systemize everything, and don't reinvent the wheel every day.

Become the CEO of Your Career and Life with the
5 *P*ROMISES

*P*ROMISE 1

I Will Live and Work a Passionate Life

Write down all the reasons you want to engage in your new enterprise. What's your payoff?

_____

_____

_____

*P*ROMISE 2

I Will Go for It or Reject It Outright

What risk must you take to pursue your bold new venture?

_____

_____

_____

Identify two potential icebergs and how you will maneuver around these obstacles.

_____

_____

_____

PROMISE 3

I Will Take One Action Step a Day Toward My Passionate Vision

Assess the effectiveness of your Strategic Life Plan. Write down the first action step you will take to make your enterprise a reality.

_____
_____
_____

PROMISE 4

I Commit to Being a Success Student for Life

What is the most enterprising thing you've ever done? What can you learn from that experience and apply to your new enterprise?

_____
_____
_____

PROMISE 5

I Believe as a Woman I Really Can Do Anything

Identify two achievements and explore how you can communicate them to promote your enterprise.

_____
_____
_____

Download the 5 Promises for Enterprise at InsideEveryWoman.com.

MARTHA'S ENTERPRISE

In 1961 I came to the United States planning to stay
for only one or two years, then go back to Switzerland.
I met Helmut, my husband, and the United States
became my home. Financially, times were not easy
back then and we had children right away. As a
stay-at-home mom I always worked. I sold Avon,
Tupperware, Amway. I sewed for some of my friends
and word got around. I became the seamstress for a
boutique. When the children were older I went into
the corporate world for a while, and I didn't like it.

Following my passion for healthcare, I signed up
for a yoga workshop, but it was already full and I
ended up in another class. Before I left Texas to go to
Montana for the workshop, the coordinator inquired
whether I would need a wheelchair. I hadn't realized
I had signed up for a Multiple Sclerosis (MS)
workshop. I didn't want to tell my husband I had
registered by mistake, so I took a chance and went
to it. The speaker, who was also an MS patient,
needed a massage every day on his shoulders and neck.
I pitched in, and he told me I was very good, that I
should do massage professionally.

I came back from the workshop, gave my notice and told my husband I wanted to be a massage therapist. He thought I was crazy, but I did it anyway. Ultimately I followed my calling, first as a therapist for about five years, then as a teacher specializing in a very technical form of massage therapy, manual lymph drainage. I travel nationwide and am well known and respected in an industry I entered by accident. Amazing what a little enterprise and massage oil can accomplish.

MARTHA, 66
MLD Therapist and Instructor

Your life is the most important enterprise of all, and you'll need one precious resource to fully enjoy your enterprise. We'll explore energy renewal next.

If [women] understood and exercised their power
they could remake the world.
—Emily Taft Douglas

What arrogance human beings have to act like life
goes on forever! Don't waste a single day . . .
—Sarah Delany, 107 years old

Plan for reclaiming your life energy in the same
systematic way you plan your career.
—Vickie L. Milazzo

RENEWAL

Reclaim Your Life Energy Through Frequent Renewal

When it's your first time, everything is exciting. Sure, you're nervous, but that's a good thing, like the way you feel waiting in line for a roller coaster. "Oh, I don't know if I can do this." Then you go on the ride and squeal, "Wheee! That was fun! Let's do it again." When you first start a new job, a new quilt, a new marriage, even the little things are exciting.

Imagine with me your first day on the job. It's 5:00 a.m. on a Monday morning. You spring out of bed, no alarm necessary. You could hardly sleep the night before, but you're somehow refreshed. You're looking forward to your 9:00 a.m. meeting, the interplay of ideas and collegiality.

You stroll into your kitchen and make a healthy cup of green tea. Your spouse comes in and flirtatiously tells you, "You're glowing." You flirt back, your eyes holding promises of something fun to come later. *Yum!* Mysteriously, your new career has even improved your sex life.

Fast-forward a few years. You have yet another 9:00 a.m. meeting—two hours of bad coffee and boredom. You didn't sleep the night before. Not because you were excited, but because you never made it to bed. You were up all night working. You rush to the kitchen, chug down your tenth cup of coffee and mentally count the Starbucks drive-thrus between your house and the office.

As years roll by, it's easy to forget the excitement we felt the first day of a new career, or just after the wedding vows or when we held our first newborn. Along the way, successful living came to mean more stress, less time and less fun.

Today's woman has taken on a wondrous carnival of life crammed to overflowing with options. We want to sample every possibility. No wonder we feel depleted. We give our all on so many levels—family, friends, career—then expect to have energy left over to help the kids with complicated homework assignments *and* still enjoy great sex. Your life is energy. Every moment of every day you're burning energy, energy you might otherwise use to pursue your passionate vision. But it doesn't have to be that way.

You wouldn't expect a battery to keep going forever without recharging. Don't expect it of yourself. Revitalize your mind, body, emotions and spirit frequently, and you'll find the energy abundantly available when you need it. Symbolically, the circle of life starts and stops with us, and women who invest in renewal have the energy to enjoy the ride long after the carnival has left town.

RENEW YOUR RELATIONSHIP
WITH YOURSELF

If you stepped back and looked at your daily routine objectively, as if it were happening to a good friend, what would be your advice? Slow down? Take a few deep breaths? Spend a few moments enjoying one day before another day crashes in with new demands?

We need to give ourselves such loving advice—and listen. We need to thrive, not just survive. To have healthy, exciting and fulfilling relationships with others, we must first have a healthy, exciting and fulfilling relationship with ourselves. Your body, feelings, mind and spirit are passengers on your journey through life. Renewal is the process of refueling these passengers. Renewed, you have the energy to accomplish your Big Things and juggle the daily demands yet feel centered, even in the unrest. Renewal lightens your load, and while the world around you may be chaos, you can remain solid in the midst of it.

Plan for Your Renewal

When you're young, you can spontaneously run off and play for a day—remember how instantly renewed you felt? But as you add layers of responsibility to your life the only way to reclaim the energy you burn is to do it with a consciousness.

Starting my business while still employed as a hospital nurse meant working extra hours. There wasn't enough time in a day to honor my commitments and also take time for renewal. At least, that's what I believed. When my energy became depleted, I drank another cup of coffee to keep going. After a few months of becoming progressively more exhausted and less productive, I had to make some changes. I wrote myself a simple but effective rejuvenation prescription: exercise, good food, quiet time and daily doses of fun.

I now plan for renewing my energy in the same systematic way I plan to manage and grow my company. I set renewal goals and strategies and formulate action steps. I schedule vacations and other Vickie-enhancing activities far in advance to guarantee that no one (including me) overbooks my calendar. Unless something urgent arises, I say "no" to anyone attempting to disrupt this schedule. For example, Monday is massage night. Even Tom knows to back off on Mondays.

For women who live passionately, a totally balanced day is not only unachievable, it's undesirable, boring. Yet I do strive for a balanced life. As I write this book I'm working 16-hour days so that I can spend 16 days vacationing in Eastern Europe. I suggest that the happiest people are the most passionate, not the most balanced.

Only you know when your life feels balanced or off balance. Your personal and professional lives are clashing and you feel little satisfaction in anything you do. Your inner fire has died. Your intuitive vision is a hazy memory. Because women are good at masking it, your boss or family may not notice you're overwhelmed when they ask you to do one more thing.

RENEW YOUR PHYSICAL ENERGY DAILY

Growing up in New Orleans, I never gave a thought to the food I was ingesting. In Louisiana, if it fits in a skillet—with or without a fight—we fry it and eat it. I also thought nothing of emptying three bowls of spaghetti or gumbo. As I grew older those eating habits left me fatigued, and my bathroom scale showed a weight gain. The habits that had worked fine when I was young no longer worked for me. I had to change my habits to reclaim my physical energy and maintain my weight. Thank God for vanity. It really does have an upside.

Physical energy is essential not only for a healthy life but for any success. It requires exercise, nutrition, sleep and a health maintenance plan. One of my friends calls me "the eating machine" because I eat at least six times a day. Yet I maintain my weight, health and energy by eating lots of fruits, vegetables and small portions of protein at each meal. I've always been a hearty eater, and I occasionally wrap myself around spaghetti and meatballs. Self-deprivation diets are demoralizing. I'd much rather exercise so that I don't gain weight every time I look at a bag of movie popcorn. I exercise six times a week, first thing in the morning to be sure I do it.

10 Strategies for Renewing Your Physical Energy

1. *Gas up.* Without being fanatical, give your body the fuel it needs. Boost your energy and immune system with vitamins, antioxidants, green tea, and ground flaxseed with natural yogurt. Sugar depletes energy—replace it with fruits and vegetables. Eat small amounts every three hours. A big mistake women make is avoiding fat altogether. Healthy fats are essential for physical energy and a strong immune system. Maintain your weight at the optimal level. Think of the excess weight as a bag of groceries you have to carry all day long.

2. *Move it.* Find a type of exercise you enjoy and do it. Create a plan that includes variety. Start with aerobics, such as walking, jogging or biking; add weight training three times a week to increase lean body mass and boost metabolism. For core

strength and flexibility, nothing beats yoga or Pilates. My favorite is hot yoga, which is a great physical workout and the most renewing exercise I've ever done. Any woman who suffers from older-age aches and pains should try it.

3. *Sleep it off.* Seven to eight hours every night is a restorative elixir. When you're sleep deprived, you'll notice a big difference in your physical condition, mental attitude and ability to cope with stress. Skip that late-night TV show and regulate your sleep schedule, which will help you avoid energy imbalances.

4. *Clean up.* When you're as addicted to coffee as I was, good strong New Orleans coffee, you don't quit cold turkey. First I replaced one scoop of regular coffee in my coffee pot with decaf, then two scoops and so on. Then I started drinking green tea. Now my energy doesn't sag in the afternoon.

5. *Rub it out.* Get a massage weekly. If that's not realistic for you, start with once a month, experimenting with deep tissue massage, reflexology or shiatsu. Manage cost by getting discounts at a massage school or by trading massages with a friend. This is renewal maintenance, not a luxury.

6. *Indulge.* Treat your body like the temple it is. Carve out a time when you can pamper yourself with a facial, pedicure or soak in the tub. Even if it means staying up after everyone else is in bed, you'll find the extra time spent on yourself well worth the investment.

7. *Breathe.* Stand and sit up straight to breathe consciously at least once an hour. Expand your lungs. Oxygen is energy.

8. *Shed your skin.* Your largest organ, your skin is responsible for much of your body's elimination and detoxification. Give yourself a dry brush massage before showering. In minutes you

feel wonderful. Start at your toes and work upward, brushing in small circles.

9. *Just say no.* Avoid depending on drugs for a quick cure. Drugs (and herbal remedies) have side effects and often detract from healthful living habits. Before getting on the drug bandwagon, seek healthier, safer alternatives. Better yet, be your own doctor and prescribe for yourself a no-drug lifestyle.

10. *Aim for attainable fitness.* Having a healthy, energetic, trim body at 50 is a perfectly realistic goal. Looking like a hot 20-year-old in those low-riders won't happen, and aiming for that goal will rob you of the enjoyment of your healthy body.

Stay healthy. Your life and love of life depend on it.

REPLENISH YOUR EMOTIONAL ENERGY

When my mom died from breast cancer, I knew I was at risk, but at only 35, after my first biopsy, I was stunned to find myself facing my own mortality. Three benign biopsies followed. I lived in an emotional battlefield, with fear impacting every moment.

Along the way, I collected the battle scars on my breasts, physical reminders of a possible outcome I could not control through vision, passion or engagement. This experience put life in sharper perspective for a while.

Then, as my business began to prosper in a big way, I found I wasn't enjoying my success as I had imagined. I was showing up edgy and grumpy. It made no sense to me. Attaining my goals was supposed to equal happiness. What had I worked for so long and so hard?

Applying my nursing assessment skills to myself as I would to a patient, I saw that I was always pushing. I had an unhealthy sense of urgency that prevented me from enjoying my life or my success. I needed time for emotional renewal.

I still have a busy life, and I enjoy a life of motion. Tom tells me the epitaph on my tombstone will read "Here lies Vickie—at last." But now I've learned to temper my whirlwind pace with occasional pauses. Even though I like motion, I'm learning to slow down. I learned this lesson from my excellent housekeeper, Thi Thu. Nothing rushes or rattles her. I'm learning from her that I don't have to be in a frantic state to be productive. Calm and achievement are partners.

To be successful and happy all at the same time, we have to be kind to ourselves. Because my busy schedule may not grant me a break later, I wake up 30 minutes early to a quiet cup of tea. In Nepal, Tom and I picked up a renewal habit called "bed tea." Every morning of our trek a Sherpa came by at dawn and thrust a cup of steaming hot tea into the hand extending from our sleeping bag. It eased the transition from our warm cocoons into the cold, thin mountain air. Today, wherever I am and no matter what time my busy day starts, I have a cup of bed tea. Starting my day with a break eases the transition from bed to boardroom.

I also end each evening with a break, reading in bed with a glass of wine in hand. My bedroom is my sanctuary, free of clutter, food and television. No matter what I've experienced that day, these quiet minutes anchor me deep in relaxation and guarantee a good night's sleep.

Being kind to ourselves emotionally includes getting away from it all. It's a challenge for me to take even a week off and not connect with my office, but I have to create an environment that allows me to escape my business, my responsibilities and even myself. I love my business, but I love it more because I squeeze out 10 weeks of vacation per year for myself. Every time I leave I come home new and different.

Women caring for their families burn out because it's a full-time 24-hour job. My mom's strategy was to wake up at 4:00 a.m., which I thought was nutty, but now I know that was her renewal time. Unless you take time for renewal, how can you not feel burned out?

Despite all I thought I knew about the value of renewal, I again became aware of my habit of rushing while biking in Puglia, Italy. Picture this: Breathtakingly beautiful bougainvillea covering a 15-foot wall. Brilliant sprays of orange, red and fuchsia against a background of deepest green—only I scarcely saw them from the corner of my eye. I sped by at 20 mph, pedaling as fast as I could to keep up with the peloton of riders ahead of me.

They were all faster riders than I, which meant I had to work hard just to keep the last rider in sight. I had to move fast, catch up, keep up and get ahead. And to think I'd come here to play, see the countryside and relax my usually rapid pace.

As realization unfolded, I braked to a stop. When Tom came pedaling back, I was easy to find—sitting under an olive tree, staring at that wall of bougainvillea. He parked his bicycle and sat down beside me. For the rest of the trip we never rode faster than 12 mph. We reveled in my discovery, not only the flowers but the peace and the emotional pace. That Puglia lesson was the best souvenir we've ever brought home.

17 Strategies for Replenishing Your Emotional Energy

1. *Get away.* Take one day off with no responsibilities, like Melissa, who assigns Saturday child-care duty to her husband, sends them to the zoo or park and enjoys a renewal day.

2. *Take a virtual vacation.* My second mom, Blanche, vacations in her bathtub with candles, bath oil, a glass of wine and her favorite CD. Maybe you'd prefer to lounge in your backyard

hammock with a favorite beverage or curl up in bed with a
deliciously light book.

Women are sensual creatures. We enjoy rich fabrics, exotic
fragrances, music, dance and art. Yet, as we reach for success
and attainment, sometimes we leave these restorative sensory
pleasures behind. Indulging in the occasional sensory banquet
is second only to an actual getaway.

3. *Detach.* When I was taking a dance class, a classmate told my
   friend, "I don't think Vickie likes me." Christine responded,
   "You don't know Vickie. She just doesn't think about you."
   Harsh, but true. I wouldn't choose to socialize with the
   woman, but I didn't dislike her. That takes emotional energy.
   Detach from emotional unrest that doesn't serve a purpose in
   your life and feel the positive-energy charge.

4. *Choose happiness.* My grandmother Pearl, who had multiple
   sclerosis, spent her adult life in a wheelchair or confined to
   bed. Yet, more than anyone I've ever known, she had an aura
   of happiness. As a child I always wanted to be around her
   because she made me feel good. While she had no control over
   her health and ultimately over her life, she saw happiness in
   every little thing, even from her bed. Decide every day that
   nothing will get in the way of choosing happiness.

5. *Be positive.* When I noticed I was wasting time thinking negatively about someone, the realization that I was only attacking
   myself with such thoughts helped me temper them. Banish
   negative thoughts and feel lighter.

6. *Accept yourself as you are.* I'm five feet two inches tall, with
   sturdy ankles. I could long to be a lithe five feet seven inches,
   but some things we can change and others we can't. The things
   you can't—let them go.

7. *Turn off the critic.* My excellent assessment skills can bring out the critic in me. I can walk into my company and, in an instant, zero in on everything that's wrong—the messy kitchen, the failed deadline. But allowing the critic to speak out would negatively impact my employees. Instead I intentionally notice some good things. When your critic squawks, put a sock in it.

8. *Practice gratitude.* For happy people, gratitude seems to outweigh desire. For unhappy people, it's about want, want, want, with little gratitude in return. There's nothing wrong with desire. Desires fire your passionate vision. But gratitude must always be greater. Otherwise, you're never satisfied, never happy. Daily acknowledge three things you're grateful for.

9. *Renew with music.* Play music that energizes you. Choose classical for intense projects. At night, play slow music to unwind and relax.

10. *Dump toxic clutter.* Because I have huge professional commitments, I try to eliminate toxic or emotionally draining relationships and other social clutter, just as I dump the clutter that accumulates on my desk. This gives me time for relationships that matter—husband, family and best friends.

11. *Lighten up.* Since I'm Italian, everything is intensely important to me. But unless I let go of some of that intensity I'm emotionally exhausted. When I find myself making mountains out of molehills, I ask myself, "In one year, will this be significant?" Lighten up. If you push, you get resistance. Be less serious about the outcome.

12. *Learn a new language.* I used to "hate" waiting in line and "hate" a bad meal. When I eliminated the word "hate," I was amazed at how much emotional energy I gained. Take all negative words down a notch in mind and voice, and notice how differently you feel.

13. *Find the fun.* Fun is healing and laughter keeps us sane. Laughter raises T-cell counts, relaxes blood vessels, eases muscle tension and reduces psychological stress, which enhances learning. Laughter can happen when you least expect it . . . if you let it.

   My sister Karen had a stroke, and I couldn't get to the hospital until after visiting hours. My dad, Tom, two friends and I slipped past the nurse's station and tiptoed into my sister's room. Just as we got inside we heard the nurse coming. Tom whispered, "Quick, into the shower!" and all five of us crowded in. As soon as the nurse left we burst out of the shower, laughing so hard we were on the floor, except for one friend who said, "How can you laugh with your sister in that condition? You're so insensitive." At that moment, Karen, who is also a nurse and was much improved, gave us a thumbs up and joined the fun by doing her impression of a gorked out stroke victim. That's when my "sensitive" friend got it. Fun happens even in the middle of a stroke. Laugh every day.

14. *Enjoy the moment.* How often do you hear or say "Thank God it's Friday"? Do we want to enjoy only two days out of seven? Why not "Thank God it's today"? Like a friend says, "If you are living for the weekend, you aren't living."

15. *Let it go.* Do you suffer from dissatisfaction and frustration? Do you find yourself whining and complaining instead of acting on your passionate vision? Try letting it all go and see the difference that makes in your day. Appreciate what you have. When frustration happens, take a breath and let it go.

16. *Create your own party.* Growing up in New Orleans taught me that you can have a party anywhere—at your house, in your mind or, as my dad says while chowing down on a good muffaleta, in your mouth. Embrace life with energy and joy. Wherever you go, take the party with you.

17. *Eat dessert first.* Sometimes we treat renewal like a dessert we have to earn by eating our vegetables. Mardi Gras taught me to celebrate before the hard work. We ate our dessert first.

NURTURE AND RENEW YOUR SPIRIT

As a child I was deeply connected to my Catholic upbringing, but after college I felt I didn't need religion, that I was happy without it. Then I befriended a woman who had a spiritually enlightened peace I found fascinating. She had no successes to write about or riches that people would envy, but she had so much more. She had a completely centered way of interacting in a world that had thrust profound challenges her way. This was a quality I wanted. I didn't want to attain success and wake up wondering, "Is this all there is?" I wanted peace and enlightenment, too, and just going to church once a week didn't satisfy that need for me.

I noticed that my friend practiced her spiritual discipline daily. I began practicing a few minutes each morning and evening. I'm still on my spiritual journey, and I'm nowhere near perfecting my spiritual discipline, but I feel closer every day.

Three Strategies for Renewing Your Spiritual Energy

1. *Quiet down.* I confess, meditation doesn't work as well as for me as it does for others. I fall asleep. My strategy is to stop what I'm doing and just be still for 30 to 60 seconds several times throughout the day, especially when I notice I'm in a rushed state. But many people I know find meditation renewing. Try it. Start with 2 minutes a day and work up to 15.

   Whichever you choose, a quiet moment or meditation, you'll feel more balanced all day and more tuned in to your spiritual source. Refuse to rely on the oldest excuse in the book: "I don't have time." It only takes a minute.

2. *Affirm life.* I can give myself a boost just by remembering what my minister says: "Life is good—all the time!" I admit that my prayers used to focus on asking for something, perhaps freedom from a health concern or getting paid by a client so I could pay my mortgage that month. Today I focus on affirming life.

3. *Study a spiritual discipline.* Whether you choose the Bible, another religious text or a spiritually uplifting book, study that discipline a few minutes daily. Spiritual renewal can be the most empowering and renewing practice of all.

RECHARGE YOUR MENTAL ENERGY

For a few years everything I read and studied related to business. I thought I was helping myself succeed. Instead I was coming up drier and drier, and my mental output was declining. I was smarter than ever, but it wasn't revealing itself in my work. Looking back, I can see that I was mentally exhausted even though I didn't recognize it at the time.

Mental energy is needed for creativity and ingenious decisions. I started renewing my mental energy by banning all business books from the bedroom, then expanding my reading to include literature, personal development books and good relaxing trash. My business grew and my output doubled.

A woman can feel mentally depleted for all the same reasons she feels emotionally depleted. When I confided to a woman from Kentucky that I don't watch TV, she said something I'll always remember: "You wouldn't feed a million-dollar thoroughbred potato chips all day long. So why do people do that to a million-dollar mind?"

How often do we feed our brains with mental garbage? We're drawn in to the hypnotic effects of television, talk radio or the Internet. None of those activities is bad in itself, but they're all negatively seductive. We turn on the television to catch a favorite show, and before we know it we've sat through hours of mind fluff. Those activities don't renew mental energy; they deplete it.

Six Strategies for Recharging Your Mental Energy

1. *Eat like a thoroughbred.* Your brain and memory depend on food to function. Eat well and eat regularly.

2. *Spark your intellect.* Read a thought-provoking book unrelated to your career. Listen to a thought-provoking CD.

3. *Challenge your senses.* Enjoy a gallery, arboretum or museum you wouldn't normally visit.

4. *Create something new.* Creating anything, whether a new recipe in the kitchen, a new product or a sculpture, renews and improves your mind. Every time we link two ideas that we never before connected, we form a synaptic bond between two neurons, and these synapses literally equate to brain growth.

5. *Take mental breaks.* I used to bring business magazines on vacation. Now I leave them at home. Long mental breaks like vacations or short mental breaks like a good movie or a 15-minute walk enable me to work with greater intensity. Work hard, but play hard and relax, too.

6. *Change your mindset.* A negative mindset focuses mental energy on the wrong thing. I'm usually on time but rarely early, and it was a big deal one morning when the hotel's room service was 20 minutes late. I was about to speak in front of 300 people, yet I was freaking out over a bowl of low-fat yogurt instead of mentally rehearsing my presentation. My

focus was totally in the wrong place. We're all human, and we're going to lose focus at times, but we need to rein ourselves in. The wrong mindset depletes mental energy.

CELEBRATE TO INTENSIFY RENEWAL

People often ask me what it was like growing up in New Orleans. One word captures New Orleans perfectly: celebration. We know how to celebrate. It's in our blood.

Most visitors don't realize that the intrinsic message of Mardi Gras is "feast before fast." Outsiders see only parades and colorful beads. But anyone living in that predominantly Catholic city knows that Mardi Gras prepares you to cope with the sacrifice of Lent.

To honor Lent you give up something you enjoy for 40 days. Knowing Lent is coming, we party hearty for two weeks. Celebration, celebration, celebration, that's Mardi Gras. Feast before fast.

What would life be without celebration? Endless to-do lists, tasks, accomplishments. Celebrating doesn't just feel good; it's the best free antidepressant on the market. The moment you experience the sweet spell of success, it's time to celebrate. Even 30 seconds of celebration colors the day differently. You can give yourself a "whoo-hoo" or a moment to enjoy the view outside your window.

Working alone in my home office one day, I completed a project I'd been struggling with. Rather than moving on to one of my next projects, which were stacked up deep, I called Tom to share my joyful moment. That evening he brought home a bottle of champagne. Toasting, acknowledging and celebrating the success together made that small accomplishment all the tastier.

How often have you reached a goal or passed a milestone without experiencing a single moment of satisfaction? If you make a habit of celebrating your smallest victories, even those that fall short of fantastic, the big goals seem more attainable.

Celebrate before the win. Just being considered for a promotion is worthy of celebration. Even if it doesn't work out as planned, celebrate your willingness to step out into the unknown. Whatever the outcome, enjoy the possibility.

Make a celebration list. Include Big Things (a weekend vacation) and small ones (a single red rose), and celebrate every day.

RENEW YOUR ENERGY WITH THE PEOPLE YOU LOVE

Who are the people you love to be with? How often do you spend time with them? When was the last time you made a new friend? Love and life don't happen in a vacuum. We need to make time and seek opportunity for expressing this most powerful emotion. Surrounding ourselves with people we love guarantees more positive experiences. It puts more life in our life.

Five Strategies for Renewing with the People You Love

1. *Spend time together.* Women who enjoy an intimate relationship live longer, and strong relationships generally require time. Share a hobby. Walk or bike together.

   Leigh has been married for 24 years, and every year she and her husband Tim renew their commitment to their marriage. At the hotel in San Antonio where they honeymooned, they reserve room 734. Their tradition begins on the balcony, where they exchange cards and gifts while a bubble machine fills the air with cheer. They toast each other and hang a wildly colorful wind sock off the railing. Later they look up from the pool and watch the bubbles and festivity happening on their balcony. Talk about renewal!

2. *Create traditions.* You've heard the phrase "What do you expect, a song and dance?" Tom and I have a silly tradition. If one of us completes a task but feels we haven't received adequate recognition or appreciation, he or she can ask for "a song and dance." The other must make up a song on the spot, along with some dance steps. It usually goes something like this: "Thomas [or Vickie] is my hero; he took out the garbage; it was really smelly. He washed out the can. . . ." You get the idea. Perfection is not necessary.

3. *Create memories.* Engage your friends, coworkers and people you love in experiences you can enjoy now and remember fondly as years pass. We all love to sit around and tell stories. Things don't bring happiness, but experiences keep giving and giving.

    Jan admits she's terrible at remembering dates, but her husband Larry is a romantic to whom dates are important. One January he called her at work and invited her to dinner at their favorite restaurant. He ordered a bottle of wine and she began to wonder what they were celebrating. What had she forgotten? Finally, he glowingly announced they'd gotten such a late start getting married they would celebrate their anniversary twice a year to catch up.

4. *Hang with your women friends.* When one of my best friends, Missy, and I traveled to Miami for a girls' weekend, we freed ourselves of work, family and responsibility. We never left the hotel grounds and did nothing but talk and talk and talk. We simply celebrated each other and totally reconnected,

renewing our friendship along with our physical, emotional, mental and spiritual selves.

5. *Celebrate passages and milestones.* When Tom and I received our bar exam scores, we took champagne and our test score envelopes to our favorite outdoor water sculpture to read the results. When we bought a lot to build our house, we celebrated on the site with close friends. Susan, the master of ritual, celebrates menopause with her women friends as each one of them reaches that passage.

Even death is worthy of celebration. Coming from a world that practiced tearful, whispering wakes, Tom was shocked at his first New Orleans funeral. He sure wasn't expecting a boisterous party and coffee cups of 90-proof "tea." Realizing we weren't celebrating that a person had died but rejoicing that the person had lived, Tom got into the celebration—and the "tea."

Celebrate every milestone in an inventive manner that creates lasting memories.

RENEW BY GIVING BACK

As author Hada Bejar said, "The fragrance always stays in the hand that gives the rose." Whether you tithe regularly, donate to favorite charities or simply make a habit of being generous to others, giving is a gratifying and renewing act. To give requires disconnecting from oneself and one's problems. Fresh perspective and renewal are the benefits.

Giving does not always mean pulling out your wallet. Time is a valuable gift. Mentoring is a valuable gift. Spiritual or emotional support is a valuable gift. It takes tremendous energy, for example, to help care for a person who is ill or has suffered a loss. Tithing positive thoughts costs nothing and benefits you as much as the people you're thinking about.

If there's something you want more of, give it away. If you want more money, encouragement or love, give it today and you will receive it tomorrow, but not necessarily from the people you give to. It comes through other manifestations. By giving back, I have received more abundance in every aspect of my life than I ever dreamed possible.

The ultimate act of giving back and energizing future generations is to leave a legacy. Parents create a living legacy in their children, and teachers create legacies in their students. Philosophers leave the legacy of their intellect, inventors leave their creations and entrepreneurs leave companies. But you don't have to be a teacher, philosopher or entrepreneur.

The legacy my mom left me is the realization that the time to enjoy life is now. Although she never traveled past the front porch of our shotgun house, she made sure that our corner of the world was the greatest. She taught me that it is a trap to think life would be better with more money, more business or more free time. We must make the most of every moment—we'll never get back that moment, ever.

Whichever corner of the world you're on, whatever you're doing there, make it the greatest corner ever. Enjoy and appreciate the important people in your life at every possible moment. If you leave no other legacy, you will be remembered for that.

SIX ADDITIONAL STRATEGIES
FOR TOTAL RENEWAL

Recognize that to live a passionate life you must attend to all of your needs, not just one or two. Energy in one area (emotional) powers energy in another (physical). Here are six strategies for pulling it all together.

1. *Set renewal goals.* I include everything in my renewal goals from maintaining a daily fitness regimen to hiking every national park. Regularly assess and update your renewal plan.

2. *Accept wherever you are in your life now and start from there.* Know that you can always start fresh. Wherever you are in life, there was "before" and there is "now." Maybe you haven't exercised in 3 years or 30. Start now—and forget before.

3. *Start small and do one thing at a time.* Enjoy 5 minutes of quiet, then 10. Add one vegetable a day, then eat two. Turn off the television for one hour, then two. Eliminate one fast-food trip a week, then eliminate two. It takes 30 to 60 days to turn your lifestyle change into a habit.

4. *Take a day off from discipline.* French fries in place of one serving of broccoli won't kill you, but unrelenting discipline will make you wish you were dead. Pass the ketchup!

5. *Banish all excuses.* I know a woman who works 80 hours a week, and her excuse for not getting away for a weekend is that she's too spent when the weekend comes. Yet a relaxing weekend away is probably the perfect prescription. Renewal often takes a little time and effort, but success and career are nothing without a renewed spirit.

6. *Create a Female Fusion.* As you'll learn in Chapter 10, this is like supercharging all facets of your vitality.

Reclaim Your Life Energy with the

5 PROMISES

PROMISE 1

I Will Live and Work a Passionate Life

What energizes you to face the day with passion? Write down
everything you can think of that renews your mental, emotional,
spiritual and physical energy.

PROMISE 2

I Will Go for It or Reject It Outright

Celebrate. What will you celebrate and with whom?

PROMISE 3

I Will Take One Action Step a Day Toward My Passionate Vision

Schedule time off for yourself twice daily. Block it off on your calendar
and write the specific times here.

Commit to exercising at least three times a week. Which days and times will you schedule for exercise?

_____

_____

_____

PROMISE 4

I Commit to Being a Success Student for Life

Study yourself for one week as if doing research. Literally journal what you do, what you're thinking, what you eat and how you feel. Which activities and foods renew and energize you?

_____

_____

_____

PROMISE 5

I Believe as a Woman I Really Can Do Anything

In which renewal strategy do you already excel? Pick one more renewal strategy and apply that same discipline. What will it be?

_____

_____

_____

Download the 5 Promises for Renewal at InsideEveryWoman.com.

LINDSAY'S *Renewal*

The Lesson of a Flower

I was talking to a flower yesterday while frantically running from the rain, trying to get into my car.

While I was struggling, the flower asked me,
"Why are you running from the rain?"

I said I did not want to be late for work,
and there was going to be traffic.

The flower asked, "Why are you rushing?

You should be enjoying the rain. It is not going
to harm you.

It only gives you a moment of refreshment.

Is this how you plan to spend your life,
rushing and running from life's beautiful offerings?"

"I don't have time for this. I have to get to work,"
I responded.

"See, there you go again. You need to stop and just look
and enjoy the beautiful drops falling from the heavens.

They are tiny gifts from God."

Before I could say anything, the flower turned away
and closed its petals.

I wanted to tell the flower it was wrong.

But at the same time I wished that I did have time to realize and enjoy the amazing surroundings life gives us.

*L*INDSAY, 15
Student and Poet

Now that you have reclaimed your life energy through renewal, learn how Female Fusion will unite you with incredible women to attain the impossible.

Every day brings a chance for you to draw in a breath, kick off your shoes, and dance.
—Oprah Winfrey

I feel there is something unexplored about a woman
that only a woman can explore.
—Georgia O'Keeffe

A fusion of women on fire is a rush of pure energy.
—Vickie L. Milazzo

FEMALE USION

Fuse with Incredible Women to Attain the Impossible

Spend a day with powerful, creative, successful women and you'll come away spinning with energy and ideas. That's Female Fusion.

Fusion occurs when you merge diverse, distinct or separate elements into a unified whole. When women come together and share their experiences, passions, visions, fears and promises, an amazing bond occurs. From that bond emerge sparks of brilliance and insight that none of these women alone, or in any other combination, could have inspired. Female Fusion is the most powerful Feminine Force of all.

According to a landmark UCLA study on managing stress, the bonds we form with women also benefit our health and longevity. The hormone oxytocin, enhanced by estrogen and released as part of our stress response, encourages us to gather with other women. The bond that forms helps to fill emotional gaps and lowers the risk of early death. Men experiencing stress go into a fight-or-flight response. Women's broader response system may explain why we consistently outlive men.

Having worked almost exclusively with women through-out my career, I wasn't surprised by the results of that UCLA study. When Tom and I were in Morocco, I experienced a spontaneous example of fusion. Our biking group interacted as couples until one night at dinner when we split up, all the men in one room, all the women in another. My entire experience of these women I had spent a week with changed during this one evening as we dug deep into heart-to-heart topics about fears, acts of courage, successes, failures and love. After dinner I asked Tom, "What did you talk about?" He said, "Sports, jokes, compared cameras, typical guy stuff. We had a great time." The women had fun, too, but while the guys were bantering and bonding superficially, the women were discussing our most profound feelings.

Yet, despite such amazing experiences with women, even I wasn't quite prepared for the incomparable results of the first Female Fusion. The Fusion that resulted from conceptualizing this book was so powerful I knew it had to be passed along to you.

THE STORY OF THE FIRST FEMALE FUSION

We gathered in a hotel conference room, women from age 33 to 72—a learning specialist, a marketing director, a graphic design entrepreneur, a massage therapist, a writer, an interior designer, a marketing creative, my second mom and me. Many of the women had never met; I was the only person there who knew all these incredible women. Some I worked with, others were longtime friends. None of us had a clue as to what was about to happen. We sat at a large, round table and began the Circle of Fusion exercise.

We each chose one of the Feminine Forces, the one that tugged at us most, then we broke quickly into smaller groups. In our small groups, one woman talked for five minutes, relating a personal experience and the feelings and memories triggered by the Feminine Force she chose. The others listened actively while writing down on small stickers positive qualities—like honor, courage, commitment, humor and joy—that the speaker's comments sparked. When the woman stopped speaking she passed her Circle of Fusion to the listeners who then affixed their one-word labels to the Circle while verbalizing how her story had affected them. The speaker then responded to each listener's feedback.

Here's One Example

Chris: I chose endurance. Endurance is seeing a light at the end of the tunnel. A lot of women suffer hard times, and when I thought about endurance, well, gosh, by the grace of God I've never had to endure anything terrible. Surviving cancer takes endurance and I've never had to do that. However, as women, we all endure. I've endured giving birth four times, and every time I said I'd never do it again. The fourth time I finally got it.

I've also endured a life-altering disease. While it isn't as life threatening as some, adult-onset asthma changes you. You have to get through it and learn what's on the other side and how your life will react to the changes. But I think sometimes we endure by choice, and that's what I'd rather talk about.

I was a graphic designer for 20 years before I became a writer. Twelve of those years I owned my business, and I loved it. I designed everything from decorated glassware to ceramic tiles, brochures, ads and magazines. I had fun doing that, but I got burned out, figuratively and literally, when my office was gutted by fire. It became an endurance to decide what to do next.

I had to continue doing what I was doing until I found a new career. You can't just toss in the towel unless you're independently wealthy. I tested a number of ideas, including writing a first draft novel, and I knew I was going to be a novelist. After folding my business, I needed an income while I perfected my writing skills, and I took a job at less than a quarter of what I had earned as a designer. I knew writing would take concentration, because you don't just write a draft and get it published unless you're a lot more brilliant than I am. During the next seven years I completed five more novels, two screenplays and several short stories.

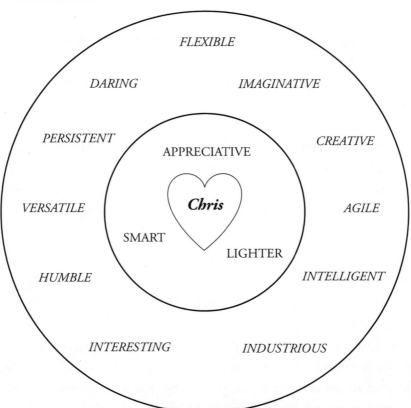

There were many days when I wanted to quit the day job. The people were terrific, but for 12 years I'd been my own boss and now I was a secretary for 22 bank auditors, so I had 22 bosses. I endured and finally published my first novel—not the first I'd written, but the fifth. I knew what I wanted and I chose to endure to get it.

Each Listener Gave Positive Feedback for 60 to 90 Seconds

Leigh: When you were telling your story, the word that came to me was "creative." It was very creative to go into a job that was completely different from anything you were talented in and allow yourself to develop your writing craft.

We continued until all the listeners had given their feedback.

Then the Speaker Responded for 60 Seconds to the Listeners

Chris: Wow, you make me feel smart to do what I did. At the time I didn't know I was being smart or creative. I just felt this was what I needed to do. But I appreciate hearing it. It makes me feel lighter. Thank you.

As every woman took a turn, this opening exercise made it possible for relative strangers to communicate freely. One woman in the Fusion described the unexpected sense of community:

"It's hard to convey how you feel when three or four women bombard you with all these positive strengths they observed in you. It was instantly empowering, a bright warmth that started inside, opening me to these women I hardly knew but who seemed to know me so well. The feeling of acceptance and community is indescribable.

"When we all came back together, everyone was glowing and chattering with enthusiasm. One woman from each small group shared results, and amazingly you felt bonded to all the women there, women who an hour ago you'd never even met. It was unbelievably affirming, and it set the tone for the whole day. We shared our closest secrets with the absolute trust that we were being heard and understood, and it was okay, it was safe."

We spent the rest of the day together at our round table, discussing the Feminine Forces, their meanings and how we use them. In Chapter 6 you read a portion of our free-flowing dialogue on integrity.

We made luxury an element of our Fusion. The hotel served a delicious lunch, plus champagne and strawberries with whipped cream. A gorgeous flower arrangement arrived from Maggie's husband Adrian, with the message "Every woman is a force of nature, of spirit, of vitality. Thank you all for bringing each new day to light."

The day whizzed by, finishing with every woman telling what she'd gained from the experience and each of us surprised by the depth of our reactions. We all went home with a glow that lasted for days, some of us lighter from unloading our secrets, others brimming with ideas and excitement for future accomplishments. Most important, we all went home changed.

THREE STORIES OF WOMEN FOREVER CHANGED

I knew that a powerful force was present that day. I felt a unique release of energy charging the air and an emotional bond that was changing our relationships forever. The other women noticed it, too. Following are three examples of the amazing results you will have with Female Fusion. You'll also find each woman's Circle of Fusion that ignited that release of energy.

Leigh: This was a beautifully planned day that didn't go as planned. I don't believe any of us expected total strangers to open up as we did. Even those of us who knew each other were astonished to see different facets revealed. The amazing camaraderie came not from talking about work or recipes but from being women. I discovered that people I work with every day didn't know what I do outside my job. I devote a big part of my life to family and organizations that focus on women's advancement.

Usually, I'm reticent to talk about myself. I concentrate on the task at hand, do it and take on the next task. As I described my commitment to my marriage, I recognized how much strength I draw from that relationship. Then as I talked about

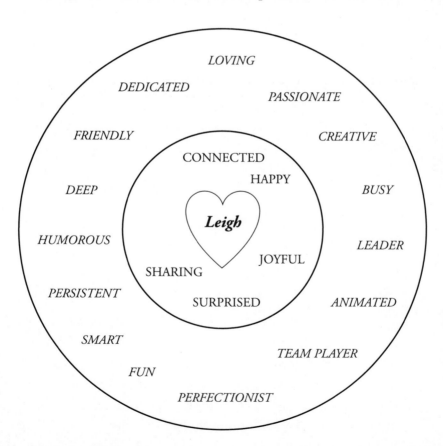

my community involvement, and these women responded with awe, I realized how much I actually do and how important it is. I left that day with a better sense of myself than I've ever felt.

Maggie: I was hesitant, knowing I was one of the youngest women in the group. I wasn't sure I had any lessons to pass on or experiences worth sharing, or whether I was ready to open up around strangers. It was also the first time I had listened to myself speak out loud, and that alone had a substantial impact on me. I heard a voice that had been muted for so long.

My family has always carried a great deal of pain for my brother, who wasn't born with the same level of abilities that most of us have. People never realize what effect this has on

a family. My mom is a strong, selfless and stoic woman who always put on her best face in spite of everything. We all did. And every day that pain was like a lead weight I dragged around, even as I centered my life around my husband and beautiful daughter.

On that day of the Fusion, one of the things I came to realize was that I had lived a more intense life than most people my age. My beliefs are very strong and central to my character. There, among strangers, listening to women share their personal stories, my heart spoke. I was able to unload some of the emotional burden I had carried in silence for so long. These exceptional women immediately understood and my heart opened. They helped me to liberate my soul and to better understand the spirit inside me. In the process, the emotional burden lifted and I felt a freedom to drive my life forward. From that point on, I decided not to live in sadness, but in grandness.

Evie: When I found myself in that room filled with such amazing women, women I respected, I knew I was there to listen and learn, but I had no idea I would leave so totally changed. During the Circle of Fusion exercise, when we all opened up to one another, these women responded to me by stating the qualities I secretly hoped they would see in me. Women I would like to model my life after saw me as one of them, and I felt instantly validated. In their eyes, I shared many of the strengths I admired in them. I remember leaving with a clearer sense of who I was and what I needed to do to get where I wanted to go.

I knew it was up to me to take the ball and run with it, so run with it I did. Although we have some amazing people at the company I work for, I started questioning why I was taking a backseat to these other professionals. I tended to go along, letting others make the decisions. Female Fusion gave me the backbone to be more vocal and openly express my opinions. That was a risky move, and I did rock a few boats.

Surprisingly, as I expressed my opinions more, people seemed to value them and me more. Since the Fusion I've received two significant pay increases, far beyond the average raise for my position, and I feel as if I can run with the top people in my company, my ideas equal to anyone's. That's a big shift for me. Personally, I feel like the luckiest person in the company.

I am truly living my dream, doing what I set out to do. During that day of Female Fusion I noticed that every woman present seemed to be living her dream but at the same time striving for an even bigger dream. That's where I see myself now.

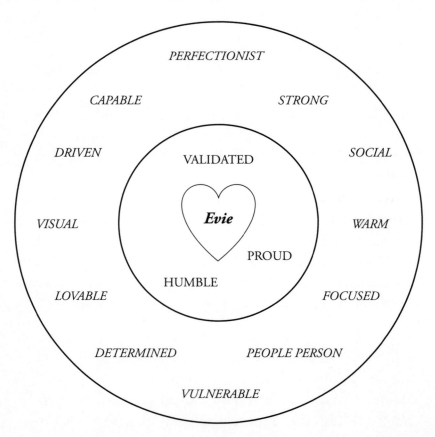

The process of collaborating, mentoring, masterminding ideas together and encouraging our individual passions and visions enabled each of us to better withstand elements that might otherwise erode our lives and careers. We received wisdom and protection at the same time that we provided wisdom and protection for one another. We are now stronger and more permanent because of our alliance.

FEMALE FUSION IS A PROTECTIVE CAPROCK

Our Fusion reminded me of the hoodoos I saw while hiking through Utah's Bryce Canyon National Park. A hoodoo is a pinnacle or odd-shaped rock pillar left standing under a cementlike cover of protective caprock.

Hoodoos are often found clustered together, an echo of the ridge they once were, and their proximity as a group protects them all from the full intensity of the elements, guaranteeing a longer life span than those left standing alone. Like hoodoos, women engaged in Female Fusion enjoy the protective caprock of the entire group. They are stronger together than individually.

As a result, when you must stand alone you are strengthened by your Fusion with other incredible women. You are at once challenged and nurtured within the safety of Fusion. You are empowered to rely on your inner guidance and to creatively adapt the results of your Fusion to your own radically distinctive career and life. We are women, and singly women can do anything, but we are more magnificent together.

Every woman in our Female Fusion gained a protective caprock, and left empowered to withstand the elements. We all wanted to hold the vision for as long as possible, knowing that we had been changed forever.

FUSION IS MORE THAN A WOMEN'S GROUP

I collaborate with women, brainstorm with women and work side by side with women daily, but Female Fusion is deeper. Fusion happens not only from brain to brain as we exchange ideas, or from flesh to flesh as we embrace, but from soul to soul.

In science, many situations exist where the sum of the parts attains different characteristics—and is stronger than—the parts themselves. For example, the metal alloy chrome-nickel steel, which results from combining chromium, nickel and iron, is far stronger than the sum of its individual elements and is used in jet engines, where other metals would melt. Female Fusion is that type of synergy but is deeper than what is commonly known as synergy in the business world.

Most of us have felt fusion with at least one other woman— our best friend, sister, mother, favorite aunt or grandmother. To feel fusion with several women at the same time is indescribable. To say you won't know what it's like until you've been there sounds like puffery, but trust me, it's true.

FUSION NEEDS HEAT

Just as you would not lay chromium, nickel and iron alongside one another and expect them to magically fuse, neither can you put several women in a room and expect Female Fusion to happen. Although it often occurs spontaneously, usually when friends share their deepest fears and wildest desires, a planned Fusion requires a coordinator and a dedicated measure of time.

Fusion needs both planned and spontaneous heat. Choose women you admire and trust, women who will pull together for everyone's purpose. Plan for a diversity of age, profession and talent. Choose women who are alike in some ways and different in others. The commonalities to look for are integrity and commitment. Female Fusion is not a "come and go as you please" event, especially if you are all progressing through the 5 Promises that accompany each chapter of *Inside Every Woman.* Every woman must commit to attending, participating fully and working through goals.

Expect to share stories of triumph and terror, brilliance and bafflement, honor and humiliation as you bond and explore your passions. Just because we know one thing about a woman doesn't mean we know everything she is. You'll learn more about every woman in your group as the gathering heats up and you laugh and cry together. Expect to occasionally feel anger and certainly to feel joy. At this deepest level, fusion happens.

You can keep your discussions purely intellectual and have an interesting conversation, but that's not Fusion. It's from a place of mutual soul-stripping heat that unbridled power and the potential of amazing reward can occur.

Expect to have fun. Female Fusion isn't serious and solemn. At our all-day gathering we shared a fabulous meal, celebrated, received gifts of praise and encouragement, strategized and laughed a lot. We all walked out of that room feeling lighter and wiser and connected.

To heat up your first Fusion, use the sample invitation on the next page.

FEMALE FUSION REQUIRES PURPOSE

While you can use Fusion in many ways, it's not a social or networking group. Everyone in the Fusion needs to have a desire to improve her life.

Your Exclusive Invitation to a

FEMALE *Fusion*

*Y*ou have inspired me, instructed me, accepted, honored and encouraged me. I want to share you with my friends and them with you in an unforgettable experience.

You're invited to a phenomenal gathering of exceptional women. We will make history together as we harness our 10 Feminine Forces:

Fire, Intuitive Vision, Engagement, Agility, Genius, Integrity, Endurance, Enterprise, Renewal and Female Fusion

We'll talk about how we can excel with these 10 Feminine Forces and encourage each other to live the passionate life we envision for ourselves.

HOSTED BY:

TIME:

PLACE:

RSVP TO: _____ BY: _____
       (name)   *(date)*

_____
(phone number or e-mail address or both)

Download this Fusion Invitation at FemaleFusion.org.

If you choose to work through the 10 Feminine Forces and 5 Promises together, you'll develop powerful goals, objectives and strategies. It will take time, but collaboration will move you toward your passionate vision more swiftly than working through them on your own. Specifically, you will engage all 10 Feminine Forces at a higher level as you:

✦ Explore your passions together, ignite your inner fires and connect

✦ Intuitively envision your individual futures and collectively validate one another's visions, no matter how audacious

✦ Engage in, and hold one another accountable for, achieving Big Things

✦ Flex your agility by diving deep into your passions and stretching further than ever before

✦ Accelerate success through ingenious collaboration

✦ Inspire the highest integrity for attracting authentic success

✦ Collectively fuel individual endurance

✦ Apply enterprising strategies to excel at being CEOs of life

✦ Reclaim your life energy through renewal

✦ Unite in Fusion to attain the impossible

After you complete all the chapters, I encourage you to start over again from your new altitude of growth and attainment. Then begin another book together.

THE BASIC FUSION FORMAT IS SIMPLE

Any time a group of people meets regularly there's a tendency to create rules, dues and don'ts. That will stop fusion cold. Yes, you need a format and someone to get the Fusion started, but you won't need officers, and you won't be inviting outside speakers.

Keep it simple. This is all you will need:

✦ Three or more women (10 maximum).

✦ An intimate location.

✦ Two to four hours of uninterrupted time for the first Female Fusion.

✦ A goal for the Fusion (e.g., complete the 10 Feminine Forces using *Inside Every Woman*).

✦ A copy of *Inside Every Woman* for each woman present. Read the table of contents and the introductory chapter on the 5 Promises before the first Fusion.

Create a safe environment where members can expose their most closely held secrets. At our first Fusion, women exchanged stories they'd never told anyone, not even their closest family members. Two things that can help to foster a safe environment are:

1. *An agreement on how to offer advice.* Only when asked for? Or openly and freely? Sometimes we need to vent our feelings without anyone trying to "fix" us. Other times we truly need and want suggestions.

2. *A confidentiality agreement.* It might be as informal as a handshake commitment that "whatever is shared in Fusion stays in Fusion" or a simple document that every woman signs.

To facilitate Fusion the first time you come together and any time a new woman is brought into the group, engage in one of the bonding exercises in the next section.

ACTIVATE YOUR FIRST FUSION

Complete one of these three exercises together before you start working through the book. For all exercises, you'll need a time-keeper to tactfully move things along and a recorder to communicate results. Whichever exercise you choose will take 45 minutes to an hour. If you have more than five members, break into smaller groups for the exercise. When you come back together, each recorder will share her group's experience.

This is not critique time. It's an informal, impromptu out-pouring of ideas and information. Keep all feedback positive.

Exercise 1: Your Most Audacious Desire

In this exercise, it's a good idea for the woman who brought all the others together to go first, because she will probably feel most comfortable.

Disclose a secret wish, something very few people know. Start with the word that most defines your wish, selected from the following list:

Love	Fun	Respect
Health	Power	Knowledge
Peace	Ecstasy	Excitement
Wealth	Justice	Fame

The woman speaking describes her wish and a personal experience that stimulated her wish. She takes a full five minutes using vivid detail. Speaking for five minutes is critical for the woman to go deep. While she's talking, everyone else jots down one of the 10 strengths that can help her attain that wish.

When she's finished, everyone in turn affirms her audacious desire.

After everyone has presented their positive comments to the speaker, she takes an additional minute to respond to what she has heard.

Exercise 2: Your Personal Promises

Take turns describing in detail one promise you made to yourself that you kept and one promise you broke. Take a full five minutes to describe the experiences that surrounded these promises. While the speaker describes her promises, everyone jots down one of the 10 strengths exhibited in keeping the promise and a strength needed to unbreak the broken promise.

When she's finished, give her the positive feedback you jotted down. Spend no more than one minute each.

When everyone has presented positive comments to the speaker, she takes an additional minute to respond.

A sequel to the Personal Promises exercise can include discussing what the 5 Promises mean to each woman.

Exercise 3: The Circle of Fusion

This is the exercise most recommended for activating Fusion. Each woman chooses a Feminine Force—fire, intuitive vision, engagement, agility, genius, integrity, endurance, enterprise or renewal. You will describe how this strength has impacted your life. It is important to choose the strength that tugs at you. Don't be analytical, just go with the one your intuition chooses. Use specific, detailed examples to illustrate that strength and how you've used it.

While one woman talks about everything the strength means to her, the others jot down positive feedback on small stickers.

You are not trying to think of something clever; you're saying, "This is what I noticed about you as you related that situation." Give only affirming comments about the positive qualities you noticed as her story unfolded, such as optimism, endurance, humor, compassion or commitment. Use as many stickers as you need.

The speaker talks for a full five minutes, then gives her Circle of Fusion to the woman on her left. Every listener in turn expresses positive feedback for one minute while attaching the stickers to the outer ring of the Circle of Fusion as she speaks. She then passes the Circle of Fusion to the next listener. When the Circle of Fusion returns to the speaker, she takes a moment to respond to the powerful insights she's just received, writing key words only in the inner ring of the Circle of Fusion. She responds for one minute relating with her open heart how their feedback made her feel.

Continue this process until everyone has spoken, received feedback and responded. One by one you'll witness the effects of the positive transformation.

Revisit these three Fusion exercises anytime your Female Fusion needs to rekindle its fire.

SPARK FUSION THROUGHOUT THE ENTIRE GROUP

Like an alloy, fusion is stronger when every woman is engaged. Here are some strategies that will help facilitate engagement.

1. No individual should be placed in authority over the others.

2. All decisions should be agreed on by discussion and, if possible, unanimity. When a consensus cannot be reached,

CIRCLE OF *Fusion*

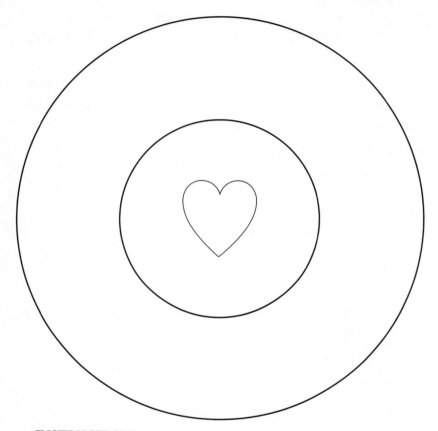

INSTRUCTIONS

1. Write your name in the heart.

2. Ask the listeners to your story to place their positive comments (key words only) on small stickers or labels as you talk, then paste them in the outer ring as they respond verbally.

3. Write your response to them (key words only) in the inner ring as you verbally acknowledge their positive comments.

Download this Circle of Fusion at FemaleFusion.org.

consider tabling the decision until more information can be collected and members have had a chance to sleep on the idea.

3. Commit to growth, for yourself and every woman in the group. It's natural that some women will progress more in one area or at a specific time than others. It's also natural that one woman will be on a fast track to external successes, while another may be exploring internal advancement. Overall, Female Fusion should result in every woman making extraordinary leaps to astonishing successes.

4. Hold your Fusion as a sleepover retreat. Book a condo in a nearby resort area or stay at someone's weekend house. Divy up the responsibilities.

5. Hold Fusions in "neutral" territory so that no member misses out on the Fusion energy by playing hostess. If a home environment is the only place available, consider rotating locales and keeping snacks simple. Some neutral meeting locales:

   ✦ Hotels, where you can often book a conference room free when you pay for lunch, breakfast or dinner. Everyone pays for her own meal.

   ✦ Restaurants that have private meeting rooms.

   ✦ A room at a church or a local club.

6. Refuse to tame your ambitions. So often we are taught as women that we should tame anything within us that is bold and affirming. In Female Fusion, encourage one another to be audacious, to project their vision way out there and go for it.

7. Ask for a volunteer to keep track of time. It's normal for some members to be more talkative and for others to listen without speaking up, but listeners need to be drawn out and chatterboxes need to be tactfully squelched. Encourage every member to participate in every discussion so that fusion will happen consistently.

UNLEASH BOUNDLESS FUSION ENERGY

Invigorate your Fusions with energy and mutual benefit.

1. Leave time at the end of the first Fusion to decide where and
    when you will meet again and the frequency of future Fusions.
    Attempting to do this or to make other routine decisions at
    the beginning will inhibit fusion. Consider gathering:

    ✦ Weekly, to complete the 5 Promises in all 10 chapters
      quickly.

    ✦ Monthly or semimonthly, if a weekly schedule is too
      intense.

    ✦ Every other month or quarterly, if members intend to
      complete the chapters on their own, coming together for
      Fusion reinforcement and feedback.

    ✦ Once or twice a year, after you've completed *Inside Every
      Woman* and want to maintain Fusion but not move on to
      other purposes.

    ✦ Spontaneously, for special needs, announcements or
      celebrations. Special Fusions can be called to brainstorm
      ideas for one individual's current and pressing goal.

2. For additional fun, design rituals to start and end your
    Fusions. You might:

    ✦ Play uplifting music before the Fusion and during breaks.

    ✦ Start by sharing results of action steps taken since the last
      Fusion.

    ✦ Start with a provocative question or statement, such as:

       ✧ When you realize your passionate vision, what changes
         will your friends and family notice about you?

   ✧   Choose an imaginary mentor, either real or fictional.
       From your mentor's perspective, what sage advice
       would you give yourself?

   ✧   What will be the epitaph on your tombstone?

   ✦   End by having everyone commit to an action step to
       accomplish by the next Fusion.

   ✦   End with a devotional, a moment of meditation or a
       theme song.

   ✦   End by reciting together a meaningful or humorous
       Fusion statement (e.g., We are women and we can do
       anything!).

3. Differentiate between critique time and noncritique time.

   ✦   Nonjudgmental sharing of important triumphs and
       letdowns, fears and frustrations, expectations, desires and
       humorous or moving encounters can facilitate Fusion at
       any time. Keep the account moving, allowing two or three
       minutes to each speaker, and keep responses brief, positive
       and supportive.

   ✦   Reserve critique time for strategizing goals, objectives and
       action steps.

4. Discuss each chapter thoroughly. Focus on that Feminine
   Force and engage the 5 Promises before moving to the next
   chapter. Your discussion might include:

   ✦   What that strength means to each member

   ✦   How she has relied on or developed this strength in the
       past

   ✦   How this strength can activate her passionate vision

5. Turn off cell phones and discourage any other interruptions. It's important to be emotionally focused as well as physically present.

6. Sit at a round table, where no one is at the "head," or pull your chairs into a circle. Or get into your pajamas and sit on couches or cushions.

7. Take a five-minute stretch break every hour.

8. Celebrate frequently. Especially celebrate one another for what you each bring to the Fusion.

9. Share your successes with other women at our web site: www.FemaleFusion.org.

HAVE FUN WITH FUSION AS YOU ATTAIN THE IMPOSSIBLE

The bottom line of that UCLA study seems to be that having close female friends is beneficial in many ways. Yet when women get overly busy with work and family, the first thing they set aside is often the time they spend with other women.

Female Fusion is an opportunity to engage the Feminine Forces in your life at levels you might never reach alone. Each Fusion will take you further and will cement your group socially, emotionally, spiritually, intellectually and physically. Expect to be together for a very long time after completing the 10 Feminine Forces in *Inside Every Woman*. You will look back and be amazed at how far you've come, and without the stress that might otherwise have accompanied such strides.

Female Fusion is such an amazing Feminine Force that I'm willing to guarantee it will change your life if you let it. In Leigh's thank-you note following the event she eloquently captured the power of this life force:

Dear Vickie,

Your vision took awesome form today. Female Fusions are now set in motion. Word of how we united through you this day will spread and grow even before your book achieves its final form.

Thank you for gathering me into an elegant place set with sparkling cool women. I am honored to be a part of this process.

Activate Female Fusion with the

5 PROMISES

PROMISE 1
I Will Live and Work a Passionate Life

Who are the women you trust, admire and respect enough to invite to join you in Female Fusion? Write down at least three names.

_____

_____

_____

PROMISE 2
I Will Go for It or Reject It Outright

Schedule the date of your first Fusion and send out the invitations. Visit the Female Fusion website at FemaleFusion.org to download the invitation and other Fusion tools. What's the date?

_____

_____

_____

Where will you hold your first Fusion?

_____

_____

_____

*P*ROMISE 3

I Will Take One Action Step a Day Toward My Passionate Vision

Which exercise will you use to activate fusion at your first gathering?

_____

_____

_____

*P*ROMISE 4

I Commit to Being a Success Student for Life

Write down one thing you plan to learn from this collection of incredible women.

_____

_____

_____

*P*ROMISE 5

I Believe as a Woman I Really Can Do Anything

What is your most audacious desire? How will you engage Female Fusion to make that desire come true?

_____

_____

_____

Download the 5 Promises for Fusion at InsideEveryWoman.com.

VICKIE'S *Fusion*

My whole life has been about fusing with women, formally and informally. The rush of pure energy that comes from fusion has helped me reach levels of success I didn't know were possible. At the office we'll stop in the hall, chat for a moment, an idea will spark and we'll move into the conference room for a crash brainstorm, or just heat up the hallway with the fire of our visions. I also fuse with my personal women friends, often spontaneously when one of us calls the other and we have a good long chat.

But the Fusion that occurred from bringing together a group of phenomenal women gave me a wake-up call to what I'd been missing in my life. It jolted me back to high school, hanging out with my best girlfriends, confiding our desires and boohooing over the tragedy *du jour.* I realized how much I missed that intimacy.

It also brought home to me how much I miss my mom. After the age of 23, I missed out on her wonderful guidance and encouragement. And she missed my important adult milestones—getting married, starting my business, being featured in *The New York Times*, breaking $10 million and creating this book. I wish she could have known Tom and all the other cool people in my life. My legacy to her is seeing the world she always yearned to see. I know she's happy that I'm living every moment and using the tools she gave me to help other women live their every moment.

I still have intimacy with my friends individually, but experiencing that collective jolt of Fusion energy was pure, soul-felt elation. My brain was sparking on all levels. Female Fusion brought me back to my mom's greatest corner of the world. I was totally emotionally and spiritually engaged, laughing, crying—caring—and the same thing was happening all around me. Attaining the impossible didn't seem so impossible at all.

I thought I had everything. But this collective force is a piece of my life that was missing, and I want it. I want more of it. And I want you to have it, too.

*V*ICKIE L. MILAZZO, 51
Writer, Speaker and Entrepreneur

Activate your own Female Fusion with the sparkling cool women in your life to more deeply release the 10 Feminine Forces inside you, and you will attain the impossible.

We are women and we can do anything!
—Vickie L. Milazzo

INSIDE EVERY *Woman* IS A LIFELONG ADVENTURE

In the beginning of this book I asked what would have to happen for you to feel absolutely enriched and fulfilled in every aspect of your life—your health, relationships, career, spirituality and finances. I hope you have found some answers to that question within these pages. I also trust that you have renewed your commitment to reach out and grab the life you crave. You already have everything it takes to get the career and life you want. And it's absolutely true that wherever you focus is where you will yield results. Focus on your passionate vision.

The 5 Promises have served me and my students well for two decades in activating the 10 Feminine Forces. I know they can serve you equally. I encourage you to embrace all the Feminine Forces within you—fire, intuitive vision, engagement, agility, genius, integrity, endurance, enterprise, renewal and fusion— through your 5 Promises. Summoning these strengths, there is no limit to where you can go.

The courage to commit to a passionate life is easily within the grasp of every woman on this planet. What I know now is when women fuse together in pursuit of our visions we're guaranteed to catch up with them. It's been my honor and privilege to share this time together. Remember the promises you've made to yourself and remember to promise big.

Vickie

For more resources, helpful guides, success stories or
to share your own Fusion experiences visit
www.InsideEveryWoman.com and
www.FemaleFusion.org

ABOUT THE AUTHOR

From a shotgun house in New Orleans to owner of a $12 million business, Vickie L. Milazzo, RN, MSN, JD shares the innovative success strategies that earned her a place on the *Inc.* list of Top 10 Entrepreneurs. Vickie's journey to success started at age eight when she discovered her first Feminine Force: fire. She was so passionate about teaching her imaginary class that her dad often had to break it up so she would play with real friends.

After graduating with a bachelor's degree in nursing and a master's degree in education, Vickie worked as a registered nurse for six years. She loved nursing, but her enterprising spirit took over. In 1982, with only $100 dollars in her bank account, she started a legal nurse consulting company. According to *The New York Times,* she "crossed nursing with the law and created a new profession."

While she built her business during the day, she earned her law degree at night. Eager to share her success with others, this innovative entrepreneur used her business experience and her passion for teaching to create a nationally recognized educational institute. The founder and CEO of Vickie Milazzo Institute, Vickie pioneered legal nurse consulting and is the authoritative educator in this field.

Vickie has been profiled in *The New York Times, St. Louis Post-Dispatch, Houston Business Journal, Houston Woman Magazine, JAVA* and *The Progressive.* She has been published or featured in a variety of publications including *Entrepreneur, Ladies' Home Journal*™, *Lawyers Weekly USA, Small Business Success,* the *Houston Chronicle, Pittsburgh Business Times, The Denver Post* and *USA Today.* Vickie has been interviewed on radio and TV as an entrepreneur expert.

Vickie built a national professional association of approximately 6,000 members. She is recognized as a trusted mentor and dynamic role model by tens of thousands of women, a distinction that led to her national recognition as the Stevie Awards' Mentor of the Year.

Vickie is also the recipient of *NurseWeek*'s Nursing Excellence Award for Advancing the Profession and her company was recognized as the Most Innovative Small Business by Pitney Bowes's *Priority* magazine. Her company continues to be recognized by the *Houston Business Journal* as a Top 100 Small Business and a Top 50 Woman-Owned Business.

Author, educator and nationally recognized speaker, this multimillionaire entrepreneur shares her vast experience and the experiences of thousands of women. Vickie coaches and mentors you to take charge of your personal and professional destiny.